Marxism as Scientific Enterprise

P.C. Joshi

MARXISM AS SCIENTIFIC ENTERPRISE
P.C. Joshi

First Published 2014

ISBN 978-93-5002-275-7

Published by
AAKAR BOOKS
28 E Pocket IV, Mayur Vihar Phase I, Delhi 110 091
Phone : 011 2279 5505 Telefax : 011 2279 5641
info@aakarbooks.com; www.aakarbooks.com

Designed by
Limited Colors, Delhi 110 092

Printed at : Saurabh Printers Pvt. Ltd.

Contents

Foreword

I first met Professor P.C. Joshi in 1972 in the office of P.C. Joshi, the elder, who was the charismatic first General Secretary of the Communist Party of India. There was clearly a great deal of obvious affection between the two, which I had earlier put down to the fact that both the P.C. Joshi had married the two Dutt sisters[1], and were probably complimenting each other on their choice.

P.C. Joshi, the elder, was a public figure and a legend in his time, but Professor P.C. Joshi (the author of this book) was not to be overwhelmed by that. He was clear in his mind that academics, not political activism, was his forte and he did not let any amount of persuasion to the contrary to change his mind. It was not as if he was doubtful of Marxism, or questioned its credentials. It was just that he had dedicated himself to scholarship first and, for him, that was his chosen vehicle for the pursuit of political ideas. Accordingly, Marxism is not just about communist party affairs, but a powerful intellectual and cultural tool. If we lose sight of this then crass revolutionaries will surely undermine the immense scientific potential embedded in socialist theory.

This volume gives ample evidence of this conviction, page after page. What the essays in this book also convey is how Marxism could have grown beyond the confines set by Lenin or Mao, had its practitioners allowed scholarly debates and

1. Kalpana Dutt, wife of the older P.C. Joshi was a legend in her own right. She participated in the Chittagong Armoury Raid along with Surja Sen and was incarcerated by the British.

discussions to flourish. There is no doubt that there were great revolutionaries in the past, whether in Russia or China or Cuba, but their experiences cannot be seen as a guide for all times. Instead, Professor Joshi sees potential in classes and strata hitherto never fully considered by mainstream Marxists. He also finds technology to possess immense liberating potential and if the intelligentsia positions itself adroitly it can use this medium to full advantage. Therefore, it is not always the proletariat that takes the lead, nor the professional revolutionaries, but intermediate classes, intellectuals and bureaucrats too, whose primary intent to deliver to the people. In this process, if it requires a mix of socialism and aspect of capitalism, then so be it!

Communism has always won in countries that were either monarchical, dictatorial or were crumbling under the weight of their own inefficiencies. What was common in all of them was a glaring "lack" and that void was democracy. This is why Marxist activists today find it difficult to function in societies where there is freedom of political expression, howsoever fetishistic or consumerist that may be. The fact remains that at the level of everyday consciousness, people can choose between rival candidates who press for voters' endorsement and favour at periodic intervals.

In such conditions, the political templates of conspiracy and peoples' war, derived from Lenin or Mao, just do not work. In fact, they actually belong to another age as they clearly "lack" popular representation, which is an absolute signature tune of the present. Professor P.C. Joshi addresses these issues with great forthrightness, candour and intellectual grit in the articles included in this book. Undoubtedly, without his intimate knowledge and analytical understanding of rural India his position would not have been anywhere nearly as persuasive. I had known the elder P.C. Joshi very well and I can say with certitude that had he lived long enough to have read this book, he too would have stood up and said "Well Done!" to his younger namesake.

It is both sad and heartening to read a committed scholar and a Marxist like Professor P.C. Joshi heave against years of sedimented hard line orthodoxy and orthopraxy. It is sad because there were not enough takers in the Left that were willing to go along with this line of reasoning; heartening because P.C. Joshi demonstrates that Marxism and democracy can be true partners in social development. As he points out time and again, there is nothing but democracy that imbrues the spirit and legacy of Karl Marx and yet it is conspiracy, cabal and violence that his followers invariably resort to. To bluff one's way out, as Communist Parties have tended to do, by calling their rule "peoples' democracy", or "democratic centralism" is just not convincing, except for those who refuse to learn from history and experience.

At the end there is calculated optimism in the way Professor Joshi analyses contemporary societies through the optic of Marxism, for all is not lost, nor has every avenue yet been mined. The uprisings in Czechoslovakia, the Allende episode in Chile and Eurocommunist interventions could all be seen as new explorations in Marxian practice, even though these attempts did not succeed in their times. Their lessons are, however, not lost, for truth, like matter, is hard to destroy. Had it been just orthopraxy then perhaps some re-wiring of party directives could help, but it is orthodoxy too which makes it so hard to go against the tide within the Communist fold.

Professor P.C. Joshi is fully aware of the many changes that have happened in the world capitalist economy and in local Indian conditions too, since the time the old slogans were crafted. Imperialism is no longer plainly visible, as in the past, but operates surreptitiously through a mix of ideological sops and economic pressure. Rural India too has undergone tremendous changes from the time we became Independent, yet these factors have not yet found adequate attention in communist literature, either in this country, or elsewhere in the world.

It is then, in the fitness of theory and method, that it should be Professor P.C. Joshi who brings these matters to our notice. Who better a person than he can there be for such a job? Nobody can question his academic worth; his scholarly contributions to caste and to the understanding of rural India are familiar to sociologists in this country and abroad. His adherence to the essence of Marxism is incontrovertible too, as is his lifetime steadfastness to the cause, in word and deed. Therefore, when he raises these important questions about Marxism they must be taken seriously. These are profound observations and can in no way be likened to attacks from the outside by sneering bystanders who have an alternative political agenda.

I have benefitted greatly by reading this book though I was never in any doubt of that when I started upon it. As I had mentioned earlier, we sociologists have for long been familiar and influenced by Professor P.C. Joshi's many academic contributions. It is impossible to get past the first post in empirical research on rural India, or on the dynamics of social relations in town and country, without duly acknowledging his works on these subjects.

Even so, I was a little surprised at how much this volume impressed me. It could well be because of my recent interest in liberal thought, or because I had never fully faced the extent to which western democracy had ratcheted up the demands made on Marxism. Be that as it may, and regardless where other readers may be coming from, I am certain that this book will be a rewarding experience for all of them.

Dipankar Gupta

1
Reflections on Marxism and Social Revolution in India*

Marxism crowns the whole movement for intellectual and moral reform dialecticised in the contrast between popular and higher culture. It corresponds to the nexus of Protestant Reformation plus French Revolution. It is philosophy which is also politics and it is politics which is also philosophy. It is still passing through its popularising stage; to develop a core of independent intellectuals is no simple task but a long process with actions and reactions, agreements and dissolution and new formations, both numerous and complex; it is the creation of a subordinate social group, without historical initiative, which is constantly growing but in a disorganised manner never being able to pass beyond a qualitative stage which always lies this side of the possession of State power, of real hegemony over all of society which alone permits a certain organic equilibrium in the development of the intellectual group. Marxism itself has become prejudice and superstition; as it is, it is the popular aspect of modern historical thinking, but it contains within itself the principle for overcoming this.

— Antonio Gramsci, *The Modern Prince and Other Writings*, New York, 1957, p. 87.

---

*This is a substantially revised and enlarged version of the paper first published in *Seminar* No. 178, June 1974.

I received comments and criticisms on this paper from a wide variety of people including Marxist intellectuals and activists. I derived special benefit from the long critique by Ajit Roy published in *Social Scientist* No. 26, September 1974 and also from the brief but sharp comment by E.M.S. Namboodiripad in *Social Scientist* No. 23, August 1974.

In my view the comments by E.M.S. and Ajit Roy do not give any indication of their awareness of the complexity of the challenge facing Indian Marxists at the intellectual level for coping with challenges at the political level.

I

The present social situation in India is conducive to an Indian cultural renewal, that is to say, to the development of new thought and culture which derives inspiration from all sources but is rooted in India's own traditions and social realities. As part of this very process of intellectual renewal, one can also sense a reawakening of interest in Marxism among the Indian intelligentsia today.

In the current situation one discerns an intense questioning of established modes of thought and practice in all spheres. This is being attempted in the light of lessons from past history of India and other countries. No doubt there has not yet occurred a crystallisation of new patterns of thought and practice. It is resisted by powerful combinations of intellectual inertia and vested interest. Consequently, the break from old patterns and the creation of new ones is yet painfully slow.

It should also be noted that in India after independence the quantitative size of intelligentsia has increased enormously. But the qualitative impact of the intelligentsia as an intellectual force is not yet commensurate to its quantitative size. The forces of anti-rationalism and obscurantism continue to exercise much greater influence on the intelligentsia than the forces of reason and enlightenment. In this background the more sensitive elements of the Indian nation are beginning to realise that the forces of unreason and ignorance cannot be fought effectively without drawing upon the rich intellectual legacy of Marxism.

This questioning mood is spontaneously pervading the sensitive elements among the Marxists also. The Marxist Establishment, however, is not at the head of this new ferment. Being immersed in the day-to-day tasks of the political movement, it is not even alive to the new mood among the Indian intelligentsia. Even today the full potentialities of a resurgence of Marxism as an intellectual force are not fully appreciated and grasped by the Marxist Establishment. This is because the traditional leaders of Marxist thought and practice have never treated thought and practice, intellectual activity and political activity, as parallel, and mutually reinforcing, movements.

They have been habitually considering the intellectual movement as subordinate to the political movement. This habit has resulted in their lack of perception of the potential of the Marxist intelligentsia as an important force for social transformation in India today. Thus in quantitative terms the size of that section of the intelligentsia which is vaguely oriented towards Marxism has expanded enormously since independence. But in the absence of conscious efforts to help the growth of Marxist intelligentsia by the Marxist Establishment, the qualitative impact of Marxism in the realm of Indian thought and consciousness is still not very deep.

It may be noted that in the field of Marxism today one witnesses a queer situation. Both inside India and outside, a renewal of interest in Marxism as a living and evolving world-view coexists with sharp reaction against the Stalinist[1] distortions of Marxism. The greatest revulsion is now being expressed against reducing Marxism into a sectarian and opportunist rationalisation of the practice of political groups owing allegiance to Marxism. A painful realisation can be discerned among a section of Marxists themselves that the scientific rigour and intellectual substance of Marxism has been underplayed by the Marxist movement. In fact, the Marxist political groups have been singularly unenthusiastic about spreading knowledge of Marxism even among their own ranks. It is no wonder, therefore, that the cultural potential of Marxism was largely untapped in the past. In contrast Marxism today has a new quality insofar as it is being rediscovered as a new mode of thought and consciousness and not merely as a political ideology.

Let it be recalled that in India Marxism first spread as a political programme and tactics of the communist groups than as a new world-view or as a cultural movement. In this context it may be noted that in India, the historical sequence of development of Marxist thought was reversed. In many advanced countries Marxism emerged and grew stronger first as an intellectual force before it spread and gathered strength as a political force. In ex-colonial and semi-feudal countries like India, on the other hand, its emergence as a political force preceded its emergence as an intellectual force. So far as the older generation of Marxists is concerned, they served both as promoters of Marxist thought and builders of a political movement. But their role as activists overshadowed their role as intellectuals. In fact, the Marxists as a broad collectivity neither fully imbibed nor transmitted the entire philosophical and cultural legacy of Marx, Engels or even Lenin. The introduction to Marxism of most Marxists began and often ended with the writings of J.V. Stalin. Consequently, the problem of integrating the struggle for power with the endeavour for a cultural renewal or the problem of creating the cultural preconditions of the struggle for power was seldom posed in Indian Marxism as sharply as it was done in the writings of Marx, Engels, Lenin and later in the works of Gramsci and Mao Tse-tung. The failure even to pose this problem led to the incapacity to evolve a concept representing the unity of power and culture as Gramsci succeeded in doing through his notion of "hegemony over civil society" (Gramsci, 1971: 271). Marxists in India never showed the mental boldness of a Mao in recognising the impact of "spiritual things and social consciousness on social existence". They did not envisage that, under certain circumstances the "superstructure" or "the cultural factors" may play "a principal and decisive role" in historical movement (Mao Tse-tung, 1954: 41). Thus in many backward countries like India the concept of politics, as both the fruit and the seed of deeper critical consciousness, did not develop as it did in some other countries.

The narrow concept of politics involved a break from the two-fold commitment of Marx, viz. (1) to transform activists (i.e. those engaged in the struggle for power) into intellectuals (i.e. into creators and disseminators of a new consciousness) and (2) to orient intellectuals towards political activism. By giving overriding preponderance to the political task, Marxists in the early phases tended to underplay the intellectual role of the activists as the theorists and ideologues of the mass movement.

Indian Marxism had a significant growth during the pre-independence period. But it did not fully develop as an intellectual force and movement in spite of its potentialities. Thinking people have asked why Marxism did not take deep roots in India in spite of a favourable objective situation. The causes of this phenomenon can partly be traced to the failure to build up an independent theoretical base of Indian Marxism. The internal disunity and fragmentation of the political forces of Marxism in India since independence can also be traced mainly to the same factor. In other words, the repeated setbacks to Indian Marxism in spite of a favourable social situation have their roots in the failure to combine, as Engels prescribed, the economic and political struggles with theoretical struggle (Lenin, 1961: 370). What was lacking was, therefore, an attempt to build up an Indian-Marxist intelligentsia on the basis of deep exploration of India's intellectual heritage and of Indian social realities and traditions. A genuine Indianness could never come either on the basis of mere quotation-mongering from Marxist pamphlets or of knowing more about other countries than about one's own country. Indianness could come only from a positive intellectual dialogue—and not just polemics—with Indian ideologues representing different or opposite philosophical orientations and intellectual perspectives. But Indian Marxists were slow in responding to this intellectual challenge.

Why is the intellectual failure of Indian Marxism so pronounced both before and after independence? Why is it that India failed to create outstanding Marxist thinkers, and a body of Marxist thought and theory suited to Indian conditions? Why is it that Indian Marxism has been more derivative than original, more theological than scientific, more assertive than receptive, and more negative than positive? To raise these questions is to draw attention to the new properties and characteristics alien to its original character which Marxism acquired under conditions of colonial and semi-feudal backwardness. This inner transformation of implanted Marxism is ultimately an affirmation of Marxian materialism itself. "It is not the consciousness of men that determines their being, but, on the con-trary, their social being determines their consciousness", observed Marx (1970: 20-21). Marxism as a form of social consciousness thus cannot escape the influence of the semi-medieval conditions of existence obtaining in a country like India.

Further, in *German Ideology* Marx aptly remarked: "Theory is fulfilled in a people insofar as it is the fulfilment of the needs of that people... . It is not enough for thought to strive for realisation, reality must itself strive towards thought" (Karl Marx, 1957: pp. 51-52). The critical, activist and creative tendencies in Marxism have often been overwhelmed in India by conformist, fatalist[2] and mechanistic revision of Marxism itself. The Marxists became hostile to questioning and independent thinking so necessary for construction of a Marxist perspective on Indian problems.

It should be noted that the mental outlook which is fostered by conditions of backwardness in pre-industrial societies has the following basic ingredients:

1. The belief in the existence of a supernatural force directing the operation of nature and society;
2. The assumption that the will of the supernatural is supreme and beyond human comprehension;
3. The control of man's fate, therefore, lies outside human intervention; and
4. The disturbance of the moral law by man's wickedness or ignorance is corrected by the appearance of avatars or the deliverers from epoch to epoch.

In Western countries these basic ingredients of the traditional mental outlook were questioned by the Renaissance, the Reformation and the Scientific Revolution. In countries like India the traditional mental outlook denying the role of man in determining the course of his own life derived much greater strength from the unique characteristics of Hindu religion and caste. The masses in India were kept away not only from property and power but also from the means of enlightenment in a far more effective and pervasive way than in other countries of the world. Further, a thorough-going cultural revolution either within religion or outside religion representing a break from these premises of traditional mental outlook was thwarted and delayed because of the ramifications of direct colonialism in India. The colonial intervention in the cultural sphere thwarted the cultural revolution directly by distorting the forms of emerging consciousness. It also distorted cultural processes by thwarting economic growth and thus distorting the process of dynamic class formation.

It may be recalled that Marxism in the West was the product as well as the continuator of the critical spirit generated by Enlightenment. It assumed the form of a higher state of man's critical self-consciousness, further affirming his heroic resolve to break decisively from the sense of his own impotence created by fatalistic forms of religion. Emancipation from this fatalism enabled man to assume *responsibility* for his own fate. "Criticism of religion is the premise of all criticism," asserted Marx. "The criticism of religion disillusions man to make him think and act and shape his reality like a man who has been disillusioned and has come to reason, so that he will revolve round himself and therefore round his true sun. *Religion is the illusory sun which revolves round man as long as he does not revolve round himself*" (Karl Marx, 1957, pp. 41–42). Marxism thus developed as a major ingredient of the critical, modern consciousness. It marked a break from certain types of religious consciousness insofar as it awakened in man a new consciousness of his latent powers and unrealised potentialities. It was a major factor for liberating him from "false consciousness"—from the pernicious influence of religious myths, superstitions and ideas about nature, and about man and society which were responsible for the darkness and passivity of the Middle Ages.

According to this reasoning man's *false consciousness* is a basic element in his exploitation and oppression in a class society. Marx, therefore, considers the liberation of man from this "false consciousness" as one of the most essential conditions for his emancipation from class exploitation. And this acquiring of new consciousness is an intellectual or a cultural task which can be fulfilled only when the suffering majority *which works* gets united with the creative minority *which thinks.* "Just as philosophy finds its *material* weapons in the proletariat, so the proletariat finds its *intellectual* weapons in philosophy," said Marx. Marxism in this way finds the chief "enemy" of the people in their own *ignorance*[3] and their chief weapon in their "critical self-consciousness". The external enemy (i.e. the exploiting and ruling class) is, therefore, strong only to the extent that the oppressed classes have not first overcome their "internal enemy" (viz. their own ignorance or "false consciousness"). By considering the development of a "critical self-consciousness" as the key aspect of revolutionary programme, Marxism serves to combine a revolutionary programme, and a revolutionary spirit with a humanist orientation. It clearly demarcates itself from the primitive-anarchist doctrine of mass emancipation through mere class hatred and class violence. It is committed to the conception of people being their own liberators through their enlightenment and self-awareness, instead of being liberated by any force, whether supernatural or superhuman, which is outside them. It is committed simultaneously to the view of the oppressed classes acquiring an intellectual and ethical superiority over the ruling classes.

The versions of Marxism learnt by Marxist activists from political pamphlets often involved a departure from the original Marxist positions. Such revision has implied that political practice is detached from the task of development of "theoretical consciousness". Consequently, it is not man's struggle based on a higher level of "theoretical consciousness" which emerges as the principal factor in the emancipation of the masses. From these versions their emancipation is expected to come as a "natural" outcome of the objective course of social evolution, as if without any conscious intervention on the part of man. And when such a "miracle" does not happen, the failure is not traced to the lower level of consciousness of those seeking emancipation but principally to the conspiracies and machinations of the class enemy. The revision of Marxism, therefore, implies an affirmation of a "conspiracy theory" of history.

The erroneous theoretical orientations of this "pamphlet Marxism"[4] have seldom been identified by Marxist activists as one of the sources of their failure to intervene in processes of social change in India with greater effectiveness. Seldom do they recognise that if a 'correct' theoretical orientation releases social energy and transforms it into a revolutionary force, a "wrong" orientation paralyses social initiative and thus undermines the active role of the people in the historical movement. It must be admitted that wrong theoretical positions by Marxist activists have been responsible in the past and also in the present for producing an escapist and perverse kind of mental outlook in the political movement, one of seeking short cuts to social revolution.

If the main reliance is implicitly or explicitly placed on spontaneous operation of 'laws' of social development rather than on man's own conscious initiative and effort; if the masses are *idealised* and *romanticised* as a ready-made revolutionary force rather than as an unconscious entity yet to acquire critical self-consciousness; if the imported Marxist models of analysis are treated as a ready-made intellectual ammunition for class war; if, instead of exposing Marxian theory to the light of Indian reality, a total blindness is developed towards those features of Indian social reality which do not readily fit into the given Marxian framework; then the creative task of preparation of theoretical tools of awakening the broadest masses to a new consciousness is relegated completely to the background. The process of preparing such tools or of creating the tool-makers is a long process, in which the tool-makers and their tools are tried and tested by people belonging to different social classes. They are rejected or accepted on the basis of their positive contribution to awakening among the people the confidence in their own capacity to shape their own present and future.

One can imagine how difficult this task of theory or ideology-construction relevant for the people is in a country like India. For India has a long history of alienation of the theorists from the people, of the absence of a positive role of people in creating an intelligentsia and of the intelligentsia in enlightening the people. This process which is fundamentally "bourgeois-democratic" had made significant headway in the West even before Marxism developed as an intellectual force. But it was thwarted in India both by the internal factors (like ossified Brahmanism and the caste system) and exogenous factors (like the impact of colonial policies). Recent Indian experience after independence has also been one of oscillation between elitism (i.e. disregard for the role of the people in the development of culture), on the one hand, and of populism (i.e. idealising the people without accepting the obligation of enlightening them), on the other. And Indian Marxists have also been guilty of this oscillation between elitism and populism as other political groups. This has, in effect, meant the neglect of the task of imparting a new consciousness to the political movement.

It is important to note that Marxism has itself been internalised in a qualitatively different way in areas of sharper break from the colonial and feudal past than in areas where the past exercises greater domination over the present in modes of thought and consciousness. This is borne out by a contrast between the Hindi speaking region and areas in Kerala. In the latter, Marxism itself made its first impact as a new cultural force as is suggested by E.M.S. Namboodiripad's *Autobiography* (1976).

In the Hindu heartland, on the other hand, both the evolution of modern forms of class structure and social consciousness were thwarted by a relatively more thorough-going colonialist distortion of the economy, society and culture. The new middle class which emerged in Bengal and the Hindu heartland in the background of de-industrialisation and pseudo-Westernisation also threw up vulgarised forms of Marxism. In the name of Marxism, forms of thought and practice developed having more affinity with hair-splitting religious theology or with nihilistic anarchism than with creative Marxism.[5]

In the next section we make a brief reference to those erroneous theoretical positions, accepted consciously or unconsciously by Indian Marxists, which have led them towards *belittling the role of social consciousness* in historical movement.

The first basic position is that of implicitly or explicitly treating "theory as subservient to practice".[6] Instead of the quality of practice being continuously revolutionised under the stimulus of a series of advances in theory, this anti-theoretical view does not allow practice to transcend the limits imposed on it by the outlook and ideology of the dominant classes. For instance, if fatalism is not questioned first at the philosophical level, it unconsciously reasserts even in the practice of a new social force which believes that it stands liberated from fatalistic orientations and values but, in effect, it is not. In other words, practice cannot become truly "revolutionary" unless it is stimulated by a "revolutionary" theory. To produce such a theory requires first the mastery of the intellectual tools created by the ruling classes in the previous periods of history. But this is not enough. It also involves the obligation on the part of the emerging class to carry intellectual creativity to a much higher level than ever achieved by the previous ruling classes. To become capable of coping with this theoretical challenge and of creating new intellectual perspectives is to achieve the first important victory over the ruling class.

The second formulation related to the first is that which regards "social history as an extension of natural history" (Karl Marx, *Capital*, Vol. I, 1957, p. 10). This premise has exercised a tremendous influence, even though unconsciously, on the thinking and practice of most Marxist activists in India. This statement has been stretched in the direction of over-determinism or the conception of inevitability of a particular course of evolution. Interpreted in this manner it misses completely the interaction of "necessity" and "freedom" in human affairs. The "necessity" of social evolution in a certain direction indicated by Marxian analysis does not preclude but presupposes vigorous social action. In other words, man's own effective or ineffective intervention is an essential element in the realisation or non-realisation of "necessity". The purpose of Marxian analysis, therefore, is not to imply that the course of historical movement is predetermined. Such implication would reduce Marxist materialism itself into a fatalistic doctrine. The revolutionary character of Marxian analysis lies not in indicating the *inevitability* of a certain direction of change but the *possibility* of it. Marxism seeks to use the knowledge of this possibility for stimulating social forces to realise it and make it a reality. According to Marx: "Men make their own history, but they do not make it just as they please; they do not make it under circumstances chosen by themselves but under circumstances directly encountered, given and transmitted from the past" (Karl Marx, 1955, p. 247). The theoretical inadequacy of the statement that social history is an extension of natural history will become clear also from another angle.

The process of class formation can be viewed as a process of "natural history" in so far as man's interaction with nature is one of the major determinants of this process and, therefore, it is independent of man's will. But the formation of class consciousness, or the formation of ideological and political forces on the basis of classes, is not a *natural-historical* process independent of man's will but a *social-historical* process dependent on man's will. While there may be a certain broad uniformity characterising the former in all countries in comparable epochs, the latter is characterised by great complexity, fluidity and even unpredictability. This is the reason why Marxist thought evolved in one country or in one historical epoch does not adequately grasp the new features of the situation obtaining in another country or another historical epoch. The Marxist theorists have, therefore, to be continuously critical and creative in order to capture these new features of social reality in diverse environments and different historical periods.

Let us consider another formulation that "the economic basis determines the social and ideological superstructure." The formulation can be found in all versions of "pamphlet Marxism" and in all popular expositions of historical materialism. This conception of subservience of the *superstructure* to the basis overlooks that the forces of change in the basis are developed and strengthened in the *superstructure*; that class conflicts (which are rooted in the economic basis) are fought out at the level of superstructure as ideological and political conflicts. Thus, the development of a critical self-consciousness—which alone represents a force capable of bringing about a change in the economic basis—requires the prior destruction of some of the basic elements of the old superstructure. In other words, it requires the creation of some of the basic elements of a new superstructure even before a revolutionary reconstitution of the economic basis has taken place and a new economic basis has emerged in place of the old. In fact, this process of the destruction of some of the elements of the old superstructure and construction of new elements in their place not only occur before a change in the old economic basis but is a precondition for generating the forces of change in the basis. The development of a critical intelligentsia as the maker and user of intellectual tools of a social revolution is one of such changes in the superstructure as occur prior to a wholesale change in the basis and even as a precondition for it.

What is the right and what is the wrong way of approaching the basis-superstructure relationship can be explored better, if we do not lose sight of the basic difference in the Marxist perspective of resolving class conflict from either the liberal or the primitive-anarchist perspectives. Marxism neither denies class conflicts nor does it idealise or romanticise them. As stated by Marx in the Communist Manifesto, class conflict has in the past either led to the "revolutionary reconstitution of society" or the "mutual ruin of the contending classes" (Karl Marx, 1955, p. 34). Marxism is committed to the conscious direction of class conflict so that it leads to the "revolutionary reconstitution of society" rather than to the mutual ruin of the contending classes". This can happen only if and when the class aspiring to be a ruling class emerges not just as a destructive force negating the past but as a constructive force carrying forward the best heritage of the past and thus tranforming class conflict into a way of achieving a higher form of civilisation and culture. This the rising class can accomplish only when in pursuing its own interest it is seen as pursuing the interest of all exploited and oppressed classes. To quote below the relevant passage from Marx:

> No class in civil society can play this part unless it can arouse, in itself and in the masses, a moment of enthusiasm in which it associates and mingles with society in general, identifies itself with it, and is felt and recognised as *general representative* of this society. Its aims and interests must genuinely be the aims and interests of society itself, of which it becomes in fact the social head and heart. It is only in the name of general interests that a particular class claims general supremacy. (Karl Marx, 1957, p. 54)

This view of developing the oppressed class as the "general representative of society" or of training it to become "the social head and heart" is in sharp conflict with the popular versions of class theory. The development of the concept of hegemony which Gramsci regards as "a great philosophical advance as well as a politico-practical one" (Gramsci, 1971, p. 333) has yet to permeate the consciousness of Indian Marxist activists. In India it has been fashionable to quote Lenin's well-known formulation that "a Marxist is one who accepts not only the concept of class struggle but also of the dictatorship of the proletariat". But the Leninist conception of this dictatorship was never narrowly political. The view that to become a *ruling* class in the political sphere, the new class should try to become a *leading* class in the theoretical and ethico-cultural spheres has generally been remote from the interpretations of the dictatorship of the proletariat as prevalent in India. No wonder that the practice based on these theoretical interpretations has been pushing class conflict more towards the "mutual ruin of the contending classes" than towards "the revolutionary reconstitution of society."

Let us explore further the Marxian concept of leadership in the theoretical and ethico-cultural sphere. A class society is always full of conflicts of all kinds which create widespread social tensions and unrest. They serve as inflammable material for various kinds of social and political agitations. Not each one of these conflicts and not every ideological-political activity based on them has revolutionary significance. And a political movement has to learn through trial and error, through advances and retreats, to distinguish between the truly revolutionary and the pseudo-revolutionary causes.

Marxism which identifies the working class as a "revolutionary" force emphasises at the same time that this class is not born with a "revolutionary" consciousness; it acquires this "critical self-consciousness". And acquiring it means to learn to relate one's immediate interests to one's long-term interests. It means understanding the "roots of one's misery", or, in other words, understanding the basic structure of society and its "laws" of motion which are linked to the long-term interests of the working class. To make theoretical enquiries into one's own problem leads the working class towards understanding its relation to other classes whose support is necessary for solving one's own problem. The narrower is one's view of one's own problem, the lesser the support from other classes. The wider is one's view of one's own problem, the broader the scope for mobilising other classes. A broad-based movement aimed at overthrowing the old social system, therefore, involves initially the creation of a wider theoretical consciousness, a *Weltanschauung* which stirs the imagination of all suffering classes and galvanises them into a revolutionary force.

From this point of view it is understandable why Marx gave prime importance to the role of a class in the production process in determining its revolutionary character. The working class alone derives its livelihood by social labour in the most advanced form of production which requires employment of a large labour force. It is, therefore, capable of organisation and mobilisation unlike the atomistic mass of peasants which is unable to unite for 'collective' action. The working class alone is capable of producing a surplus over and above its subsistence (via Marx's distinction between labour and labour power). The revolutionary potentialities of this class, therefore, stand in sharp contrast to the reactionary character of those classes (like landlords, traders, usurers, etc.) which are mere appropriators of the surplus; or to the limited revolutionary potential of those classes (like capitalists) whose conditions of existence do not allow the full mobilisation of the surplus and, therefore, the full release of the productive forces; or to the semi-revolutionary character of those (like the peasants and artisans) whose conditions of existence keep the size of this surplus restricted to an absolutely low level. The working class alone is fully rooted in the productive process and has no roots in the structure of private property. It alone represents a genuinely dynamic force in the economy and consequently a force capable of a consistently revolutionary role.

II

Distortions of Class Formation and Ideological and Political Forms

The implications of this Marxian view of class would become clear as we take account of the important features of class formation in transitional societies like India. Here the traditional economy has reached an advanced state of disintegration without, however, making the transition to an industrial economy characterised by a high level of development of productive forces. One of the typical features of such economies is the proliferation at the top, middle and bottom of the class structure of such classes and social strata as do not have any positive relation to the process of production. They are a parasitic force in the economy and a corrupting or disintegrating force in the polity. Marx noted the existence of these classes in the economy and their pernicious role in the polity in his analysis of the *Class Struggle in France* (1948-50), in the *Eighteenth Brumaire of Louis Bonaparte* (1852), and Engels did the same in his work on *The Peasant War in*

Germany (1850). Mao Tse-tung has also noted similar features in China. One of the weaknesses of the Indian Marxists has always been that in their class analysis of India they have missed all such crucial and distinctive features of class formation as have an important bearing on the peculiarities of Indian ideological and political development.

Marx drew attention to the fact that "capital's secondary modes of exploitation" (Karl Marx, 1955, p. 149) like speculation and usury were more predominant than the capitalist mode of production in France of 1848-50. This meant the stranglehold of a "financial aristocracy" over the economy which was obsessed by the "mania to get rich"—to get rich not by production but by "pocketing the already available wealth of others." Karl Marx continues:

> Clashing every moment with bourgeois laws themselves, an unbridled assertion of unhealthy and dissolute appetites manifested itself, particularly at the top of bourgeois society—lust wherein wealth derived from gambling naturally seeks its satisfaction, where pleasure becomes debauched, where money, filth and blood commingle. *The financial aristocracy in its mode of acquisition as well as its pleasure is nothing but the rebirth of the lumpen proletariat on the heights of bourgeois society.* (Karl Marx, 1955, p. 142).

We quote this passage because it sums up so well an important feature of the class situation at the top of the class structure even in countries like India.

And what is the lumpen proletariat? Engels observes:

> The *lumpen* proletariat, this scum of the deprived elements of all classes, which establishes its headquarters in the big cities, is the worst of all possible allies. The rabble is absolutely venal and absolutely brazen. If the French workers in every revolution, incribed on the houses, *Death to Thieves*, and even shot some, they did it, not out of enthusiasm for property but because they rightly considered it necessary above all to keep that gang at a distance. Every leader of these workers who uses these scoundrels as guards or relies on them for support proves himself by this action alone a traitor to the movement. (F. Engels, 1956, p. 14).

Mao in his analysis of classes in Chinese society (1939) noted the existence of the "vagrants" as an important social category in the Chinese countryside and the cities. His observations on their role are extremely relevant:

> China's colonial and semi-colonial status has created a multitude of unemployed people both in the countryside and the cities. Denied any legitimate way of making a living many of them are forced to revert to illegitimate means, hence the robbers, the gangsters, beggars, *prostitutes* and all those who live upon superstitious practices. Lacking the constructive quality and given more to destruction than to construction, these people after joining the revolution become the source of the ideology of the roving insurgents and of anarchism among the ranks of the revolution. Therefore we should know how to remould them and forestall their destructiveness. (Mao Tse-tung, 1954, p. 95).

At the top, middle and lower levels of the state structure also there is an over-expansion of unproductive or semi-productive social strata connected with the vast governmental, semi-governmental and military establishments. In the *Eighteenth Brumaire of Louis Bonaparte* Karl Marx describes the wide ramifications of the state machine and its numerous forms of dominance over civil society. The following observations made for the French society are equally relevant for India today.

> This executive power with its enormous bureaucratic and military organisation, with its ingenious state machinery, embracing wide strata, with a host of officials numbering half a million, besides an army of another half million, this appalling parasitic body, which enmeshes the body of French society like a net and chokes all its pores, sprang up in the days of the absolute monarchy, with the decay of the feudal system, which it helped to hasten. The seignorial privileges of the landowners and towns became transformed into so many attributes of the state power, the feudal dignitaries into paid officials and the motley pattern of conflicting medieval plenary powers into the regulated plan of a state authority whose work is divided and centralised as in factory... . Every *common* interest was straightaway severed from society, counterposed to it as a higher,

> general interest snatched from the activity of society's members themselves and made an object of government activity, from a bridge, a school house, and the communal property of village community to the railways, the national wealth and the national university of France... All revolutions perfected this machine instead of smashing it. The parties that contended in town for domination regarded the possession of this huge state edifice as the principal spoils of the victor. (Marx, 1955, pp. 332-33).

Attention should also be focussed on the educated social strata being created by the proliferating centres of higher education and reasearch, serving as manufacturies of ill-trained, over-ambitious and unemployed or semi-employed youths. These social strata are denied a positive outlet for their energies and thus constitute a repository of seething dissatisfaction and rebelliousness without content or direction. They can be termed a *lumpen middle class* on account of their social rootlessness. The disciplining of this social category is the hardest problem facing most underdeveloped countries. But until society has evolved a positive framework for absorbing them as a constructive force, the threat posed by them to the social order increases day by day. This necessitates tremendous increase in the expenditure on the police force and other mechanisms of coercion and repression. This means further prolieration of social strata alienated from productive work and living at the expense of those engaged in productive activity.

In a nutshell, in transitional societies like India the 'financial aristrocracy', the government and military bureaucracy, the lumpen middle class and the *lumpen* proletariat are the typical unproductive social categories which seem almost to *over-shadow the productive classes like the genuine industrial and agricultural entrepreneurs, the skilled intelligentsia, the toiling peasants and the working classes. This block of the unproductive classes obstructs the formation and consolidation of a block of the productive classes.* These unproductive classes are also the vehicles of two perverse psychological drives viz., *avarice* (i.e. the mania to get rich), on the one hand and *envy* (i.e. the craze to ape the rich or to pull them down to one's own level), on the other.

Avarice and *envy* are thus the sources of two major tendencies of contemporary social movements, the tendency of parasitic *economism*, on the one hand, and primitive rebelliousness and anarchism, on the other. While these are found in the most concentrated form in the 'financial aristocracy', the lumpen middle class and the 'lumpen proletariat', they infect all other classes of society, including the working class. What are idealised even by the radicals as class conflicts are thus conflicts not between one class combination committed to sectional interest and another to the interest of the whole society; not between one representing parasitic appropriation of the economic surplus and another representing enlargement of this surplus so as to raise the level of social productivity; not between one representing a low level of social ethics and culture and another representing a much higher level. The compulsive force of avarice seems to be leading all social classes now towards aggressive competition in parasitic economism; and when avarice is thwarted, the compulsive force of envy generates moods of primitive rebelliousness and in such moods the *lumpen* proletariat is the most active force subjecting society occasionally to a mad orgy of primitive terror, arson, loot and violence. Both these tendencies use socialism as an ideological disguise, one thriving under the guise of 'distributive socialism' and the other under the guise of 'militant' and 'extremist' socialism.

Both these orientations are, however, alien to the Marxist concept of social revolution. As Marx stated very clearly in his *Economic and Philosophical Manuscripts*:

> General *envy* constituting itself as a power is the disguise in which *avarice* re-establishes itself and satisfies itself, only in *another way*. The thoughts of every piece of private property—inherent in each place as such—are *at least* turned against all *wealth* and private property in the form of envy and the urge to reduce to a common level, so that this envy and urge even constitute the essence of competition. The crude communism is only the consummation of this envy and of this levelling down proceeding from this preconceived minimum. How little is this annulment of

> private property really an appropriation is in fact proved by the abstract negation of the entire world of culture and civilisation, the regression to the *unnatural* simplicity of the poor and *undemanding* man who has not only failed to go beyond private property, but has not yet even attained to it. (Karl Marx, 1844, p. 100).

It is necessary to draw attention to such changing material conditions of a transitional society as feed the drives of avarice and envy and convert them into explosive forces. These find expression in diverse forms of ideology and politics.

(1) A society in transition like India is subject to continuous "dislocation and break with the old order" with the result that "substantial portions of the population are dislodged from their accustomed pursuits and from the established and entrenched sectors of the old economic order" (Simon Kuznets, 1969, p. 106). Thus economic and political changes lead to considerable downward mobility of the old leisured classes which enjoyed privileged positions in the princely order, in the *Zamindari* and the *Jagirdari* systems, and in the old colonial regime. These dethroned aristocracies of the old order do not easily give in when exposed to serious troubles and turmoils of the transition period. They tend to rally behind themselves all the discontented strata at the lower levels of society and thus emerge as leaders of aggressive pressure groups or bandit gangs or even mass movements. They may hide their real interests behind revivalist or radical slogans. They may be the leaders of markedly obscurantist politics or of *feudal socialism*. This is a term which is used by Marx in the *Communist Manifesto* to characterise the radicalism of the feudal class (Karl Marx, 1955, pp. 54-55). It is a type of socialism which is "half lamentation, half lampoon; half echo of the past, half menace of the future; at times by its bitter, witty and incisive criticism, striking the bourgeoisie to the very heart's core but always ludicrous in its effect, through its incapacity to understand the march of history" (Ibid.)

Feudal Socialism, however, may succeed in capturing the minds of discontented masses in the absence of any alternative path and on account of their cultural backwardness and, therefore, their vulnerability to obscurantist appeals. Feudal socialism is, however, nothing more than avarice of the old ruling class turned into envy as their position is seriously undermined by the emerging economic classes of Kulaks, on the one hand, and usurious, and industrial capital, on the other.

(2) The forces of change undermine the old stability also of bottom groups like the peasants, the artisans and the small traders, etc. The uprooting of these from their traditional positions of security does in fact proceed much faster than their absorption in the modern sectors of the economy. These uprooted groups are left hanging *Trishanku-like* in the air; they lose the old world without the gain of a new one. The swelling numbers of this uprooted mass from the rural to the urban scene adds further to their smouldering resentment and discontent. They provide the soil for social protests which at the slightest provocation turn into violent outbursts. These may take the shape of communal, casteist or regional tensions, and of anti-social acts like thieving, burglary, incendiarism, rapes, murders, rowdyism and hooliganism of all varieties. They contribute to the underworld of crime in all big cities and towns. The major driving forces of these groups are their hatred and envy of the privileged and the affluent. And the growth of the *lumpen bourgeois* at the top also invariably implies the growth of an embittered *lumpen-proletariat* at the bottom.

The accumulation of wealth through spoils and the rage against it go together. The callous indifference shown by the rich living in the palaces to the slum-dwelling underdogs in their very neighbourhood is the souce of hatred which smoulders in the minds of the poor against the rich rolling in luxury. This hatred for and envy of the rich, which is the basic motivation of the lumpen proletariat, often creates an illusion as if it is a force for socialism. But it is, in effect, a force which disintegrates the socialist movement rather than strengthens it. Some of the characteristics of socialist groups in India—e.g. the equation of socialist propaganda with mere exposure of scandals and intrigues among the ruling classes, the revelling in the use of abusive language in exposure campaigns, the frequent resort to character-assassination as a political technique and concentration on personalities rather than on issues—can be understood only if they are related to the lumpen-proletarian social base of these groups. Nothing satisfies the lumpen-proletarian psychology more than the act of denigrating those who are entrenched in positions of power and affluence and in attempting to pull them down to their own level through mud-slinging vituperation, intrigues or hoolinganism. Destructive rage emanating from envy finds its major ideological expression in this brand of socialism, *lumpen-proletarian socialism*, which is another name for primitive anarchistic form of socialism.

(3) The third important social stratum which multiplies and gains continuous prominence in underdeveloped countries is the middle class. The urbanisation of the country without adequate industrialisation pushes this middle class into all sorts of activities of the tertiary sector including the political sector. The main thing here is the gap between the rising aspiration level of these classes whose consumption appetites are over-stimulated by continuous propaganda from affluent countries, and the thwarting of these aspirations due to low level of material development of the country. The craze for easy success leads members of this class towards social instability and political dissatisfaction. These find an outlet in both right and left political orientations. In the case of this middle class *envy* takes the ideological form of populist or middle *class socialism*. While the diversion of the national resources towards middle class luxury production—small cars and refrigerators, air-conditioners, posh residential colonies, modern means of private recreation, five star hotels, etc.—is one of the chief objectives of this brand of socialism, bargaining pressure, manipulative politics and frequent use of money power, are its chief instruments. This class is most satisfied with the parliamentary path of socialism which it has reduced into a path of pressure, bargaining, buying and cajoling. The middle class—aptly christened as the *nouveaux*

riches—provides the most important recruiting ground for all members of legislature, parliament and political parties of all complexions. Middle class socialism is at the moment the most important ideological force in Indian politics.

(4) We now turn to the peasant whose response to the impact of modern forces constitutes "a strange mixture of reaction and revolution, of superstition and shrewd estimate of class interest". The peasant has a Janus-like character, both forward-looking and backward-looking at the same time. The peasantry's hatred of feudal landlordism and urban capitalist dominance—which explains its responsiveness to forces of change and its frequent outbursts of rebelliousness—is combined with a literal acceptance of religious doctrines emphasising passive resignation and "a childlike belief in the protection of miralce-working saints" which explains its social and political passivity. This means that the peasants' interest does not assume the form of a well-defined, integrated and independent ideology. Ideologically the peasantry oscillates between conservatism on larger questions of modernisation, on the one hand, and of radicalism on the land question, on the other. It is sometimes the ally of the feudal and at other times of the *lumpen*-proletarian and other forms of socialism. Politically the peasantry leans towards total passivity interrupted by "passive" support to parliamentry politics or, in extreme cases, by outbreaks of rebelliousness.

In a country where the peasantry constitute the dominant social group, politics for a long time takes the form of politics by bands of "volunteers" and "activists" on behalf of the peasantry rather than by the peasants themselves. While the peasants' lack of access to means of culture and enlightenment predisposes them to lack of consciousness, their atomistic character predisposes them to lack of organisation. It reduces them to passivity and makes them seek paternalistic protection from other groups who monopolise culture and power (the bourgeoisie or the middle class) or to those who have the capacity for organisation (the working class). In transitional societies the peasant has no ideology of his own but is drawn towards ideologies of a contradictory character, from Hindu socialism and Sarvodaya or parliamentarism at one end to Naxalism at the other.

(5) We now turn to the working class. The two most important characteristics of the working class in transitional societies like India, which condition its ideological and political orientation can be noted. The first is the small size of the working class insofar as it is outnumbered by the peasants and also by the vast masses of the urban and rural poor who are *pauperised* but not *proletarianised* (i.e. they do not live by wage labour). The second important feature is that it is to a large extent of peasant origin and has not yet broken its umbilical cords with the peasantry and the village. Exposed to the overwhelming forces of the peasantry and the lumpen-proletariat, from whom it has originated, the new working class suffers from the narrow horizons and backward orientations of the peasants, at one end, and the anarchic moods of *lumpen* proletariat, at the other. On the basis of the former it is extremely susceptible to the appeals of communalism, casteism, militant regionalism and other forms of fanaticism. On the basis of the latter arises its recurrent disregard for the rules of the game implicit in an industrial economy and society as reflected in unplanned stoppages or slowdown of work in the power plants, the railways, the steel plants and other vital branches of social economy. Even in the socialist countries the degeneration of socialism into *bureaucratism* is said to have been facilitated by the new working class whose peasant origin still weighed on its psychology. Such a working class has been the inevitable social base of *bureaucratic socialism* in many Asian countries including India.

We have so far discussed the ideological forms of socialism in India in which the basic motivations of avarice and envy get crystallised expression. These forms serve the needs of the parasitic or the semi-parasitic bloc of classes which has emerged as a powerful constraint on India's growth and development since independence. Corresponding to these ideological forms are the forms of politics characteristic of this parasitic bloc which also deserve to be noted. The political resilience of this parasitic bloc is ensured only if the "apoliticism and passivity" of the broad masses is ensured and maintained. Politics related to the perverse forms of socialism mentioned above, therefore, assume forms "not of actions and organisations of homogeneous social blocks" but "of actions and organisations of volunteers". This distinction made by Gramsci is extremely important for understanding the nature of present-day politics in India and for indicating the required direction of change. By "volunteers" are meant those who, according to Gramsci, are not "an organic expression of the social mass but rather those who have detached themselves from the mass by arbitrary individual initiative and who often stand in opposition to that mass or are neutral with respect to it" (Gramsci, 1971, p. 203). As a result, this form of politics substitutes the activity of the "volunteers" for the activity of the broad masses; it substitutes, the heroism of the "volunteers for the heroism of the masses".

It must be pointed out that political parties themselves when they get disoriented from their social and ideological moorings also resemble a rootless band of volunteers living at the expense of the masses rather than a broad-based political force rooted in the masses and continuously interacting with them.

Such politics of "voluntarism", therefore, may serve to reveal the imbalances and contradictions of the social system. But it can never serve as an agent of change in the social system. For such change the broad masses have to be educated and activised and a homogeneous and compact social bloc has to be created. To stimulate the formation of such a bloc and to release the energies of the broad masses requires the creation of a new type of intellectuals and activists not separated from the masses but organically linked with the masses. These intellectuals can be effective only if they try to create new normative principles or ideological orientations which embody the fundamental interests of the bloc of productive classes and social strata at all stages of the transition; and which by stirring their imagination, serve to detach them from the perverse ideological orientations propagated by the bloc of the unproductive classes and social strata.

III

The Intellectual Renewal of Marxism and the Process of Indian Cultural and Political Renewal

It must be recognised that this process of creation of new normative principles, of the development of intellectuals as the creators and disseminators of these principles and of the formation and consolidation of a bloc of the productive classes has gone by default since independence. *This entire process may be termed as the generation of the cultural forces of a social revolution.* It must also be recognised that these cultural forces which were generated and consolidated under the leadership of Gandhi and Nehru for the anti-imperialist struggle and for the creation of a bloc of anti-imperialist classes as an instrument of this struggle disintegrated after the achievement of independence. They were not adequate for this post-independence period. The disintegration of the inherited cultural forces and the failure to build new forces is at the root of most of the political chaos and social disruption that one finds in India today. The vacuum created by this default is filled up by perverse ideological orientations corresponding to the baser instincts of man and the vulgar forms of politics based on them which have dominated Indian social and political life in recent years.

This process of disintegration of inherited cultural forces has also pervaded Indian Marxism which has also been pressed into the service of nihilist ideology and pseudo-revolutionary practices. As we explained earlier, the task of building up an intellectual base had been neglected by Indian Marxists in the pre-independence period. These Marxists used Marxism mainly as a political tool rather than as an intellectual tool for generating a new consciousness. *Indian Marxism can regenerate itself as a creative force only by addressing itself to the task of development of the new cultural forces of the Indian revolution.* This task has three basic aspects: (1) the scientific critique of the old principles and the reformulation of the *new normative principles* suited to the present stage of the Indian revolution; (2) the dissemination of these principles among the broadest masses and productive classes of Indian society; (3) the concretisation of these new normative principles in programmes and strategies of change in the economic, social and political institutions which thwart the realisation of these principles; (4) and lastly, the consolidation of a bloc of the broadest masses and of the productive classes through appropriate forms of political struggle and mobilisation with a view to getting these principles implemented.

Let it be clearly stated that no single Indian ideology—neither old Gandhism nor neo-Gandhism, neither old Nehruism nor neo-Nehruism, neither Indian Marxism (of all shades) nor any other ism—is by itself capable of undertaking this task of generating the new cultural forces. The positive dialogue between all these forces—a courageous and honest attempt on the part of every trend to reexamine its own premises in terms of actual experience of the last twenty-five years—alone can prepare the ground for a new synthesis relevant to the present needs of the Indian situation. Marxism will be an important contributor to this new unifying framework. But this framework or synthesis cannot be created by Marxists alone without a positive dialogue with Gandhites and Nehruites and Indian socialists.

Before we indicate the potentialities of Marxism in this task, we must indicate the inadequacy of present-day Western ideological orientations which our intelligentsia has imbibed since independence. It is not the synthesising and critical approach of the Renaissance to which our intelligentsia has been exposed in the recent period. It is the divorce of one branch of knowledge from another, of knowledge from life and of the creators of knowledge from the people, which constitutes the intellectual legacy of the latter half of the twentieth century from the Western (primarily American) world to the underdeveloped countries. This legacy has contributed to the fragmentation of the intellectual forces, the alienation of one section of the intelligentsia from another and of the intelligentsia as a whole from the people which we witness in India today. No wonder that this intelligenstia has not been able to detach itself from the bloc of unproductive and parasitic class to which we drew attention earlier. And if the intellectuals have to emerge as one of the most important forces in the new bloc of the broad masses and other productive classes, they have to be the first to break from the old habits of thought and approaches in comprehending and coping with the present Indian problem. In breaking from these orientations one has to draw upon Marxism which has its roots in the Renaissance traditions of the unity of knowledge, on the one hand, and of knowledge and action, on the other. At the same time, Indian Marxism has also to overcome its basic weaknesses if the potentialities of Marxism for creating the cultural forces of the Indian revolution are to be realised.

First of all it must be recognised that the original orientation of Marxism is hostile to the conversion of the intelligentsia into a highbrow technocracy or a priesthood alienated from the people. Indian Marxism in the past failed to develop alone this original orientation. In fact, Marxism in India was Indianised in the wrong sense. Instead of being accepted as a philosophy of *praxis*, it turned often into the status symbol of a caste of neo-Brahmans. For did the Marxists not re-emerge as a new caste of Indian Brahmans endlessly engaged in sterile and hair-splitting debates in a language which they alone understood and which alienated them increasingly from living communication and interaction with the Indian people? That the top Marxists thought, wrote and communicated with one another not in the language of the people but in a foreign language was another basic factor why Marxism was not Indianised in the right sense. It neither acquired full rootedness in Indian social realities nor did it become a force in the consciousness of the common people to whom it really belongs. That is the reason why many vital features which are specifically Indian have eluded the Indian Marxists; the specific has always been lost in the broad generalities. Some of these questions specific to the Indian situation like the religious factor, caste and untouchability, the woman question, tribal problems, problems of nationality and ethnic groups, the language issue, multiclass nationalism, the problems of the peasantry and the role of charismatic individuals like Gandhi—have yet to be studied by the Indian Marxists. No wonder that Indian Marxism has a derivative character. Its failure to deal with Indian social reality has found its chief expression in the total neglect of India's history, culture or traditions. Insofar as India's present and future, cannot be understood or remoulded without an understanding of the forces which have shaped India's past history, a lack of such understanding has not allowed Indian Marxists either to communicate with Indians or to release the forces of social change in India. D.D. Kosambi is one of the few outstanding Marxist intellectuals who tried to study Indian history on the basis of the Marxist approach.

It should be emphasised that Indian Marxism has a wealth of practical experience to its credit. But it has lacked so far the orientation and capacity to derive stimulus from this experience for formulating questions and constructing theories relevant to the Indian situation. The lack of assertion of intellectual independence and the respect for its own experience has made Indian Marxism imitative and "unIndian"—sometimes a caricature of Stalinism and sometimes of Maoism. Indian Marxism has yet to create its own Karl Marx, or Lenin or Mao who is able to integrate the general orientation of Marxism with the specific realities of the Indian situation. And this regeneration of Indian Marxism cannot take place unless it is willing to respect, understand, critically assimilate and then transcend all the vital movements and orientations produced by Indians in the remote and the recent past.

An Indian Marxist who has crammed all the works of Lenin or Mao but has not cared to study and grapple with Gandhi's thought and practice can never hope to contribute anything relevant to the Indian situation. The general contempt which Indian Marxism has exhibited for Gandhi is only a reflection at its roots of the contempt of an urban middle class for the village-dwelling Indian peasantry. The distance of Indian Marxism from Gandhi is essentially a reflection of its distance from the Indian peasantry. Let it be noted that most of the outstanding Indian Marxists are a product of this urban middle class and quite a few of them have been trained in Western universities. The claim of this middle class to be emancipated from backward ideologies like Gandhism has in effect resulted in its "emancipation" from Indian reality itself. For, Gandhi typifies this peasantry with its Janus-like character. And not to understand Gandhi is to remain ignorant of the complex problems of activating the Indian peasantry. Gandhi's historic contribution was to draw this peasantry into the freedom movement. *The problem today is to draw the peasant into the mainstream of modern development and socialist transformation*. Even though Gandhism is not adequate to the present task, the intellectual basis for coping with this cannot be created without assimilating critically the heritage of Gandhian thought and practice.

Indian Marxism faces its toughest intellectual challenge in the peasant problem—the problem of comprehending the nature of the peasant economy, society and culture and the problem of enlightening the peasant and activising it is a political force. It is a task which calls for multi-disciplinary synthesis. In the last 25 years social scientists belonging to different disciplines have taken up the study of the village from the perspective of different disciplines. The anthropologists have contributed numerous village studies dealing with the social system of the village and with the social life of the tribes and the peasants. The economists have studied the economics of agriculture and the problems of rural economic development. The political scientists have taken up surveys of the political processes and the political institutions in Indian villages. The official and non-official agencies have contributed an enormous mass of data relating to the village economy and society the like of which was never collected before. The utilisation of this massive data and insights for construction of a new theoretical perspective of the peasant problem and of a strategy of modernisation of the peasantry remains an unfulfilled task. Indian Marxists can contribute significantly to the fulfilment of this intellectual task. They have, however, not yet addressed themselves to this problem. In fact, their failure to enter into a fruitful dialogue with social scientists and to draw upon social science is one of their basic failures which has been recognised by E.M.S. Namboodiripad in the following words:

> I should also mention here that a feeling has of late grown within me that those of us who have been engaged in heated debates on the problems connected with the socialist pattern have been doing so without digesting the material collected and conclusions drawn by a host of scholars and research workers in the field of social science. Our failure in this respect is, I believe, one of the major reasons why we are unable to make a proper evaluation of the actual developments taking place in the country, and on its basis to unify the patriotic, democratic and socialist forces in the country. (1966, p. viii).

Namboodiripad's statement provides a refreshing contrast to the general scepticism about, if not hostility to, professional social science which characterises the political activists in India. But even Namboodiripad's statement does not go far enough in recognising how the abandonment of a scientific approach has been responsible for the intellectual ossification of Indian Marxism and its failure to intervene effectively in the Indian situation.

In this background an intellectual renewal of Indian Marxism alone holds the key for its political renewal as well. An intellectual renewal alone can bring about a decisive break from the fatalistic Marxism of the last 25 years which denies any responsibility for failure to intervene effectively in Indian problems in general and the peasant problem in particular. Such fatalistic Marxism sees in the conspiracy of the ruling class the main cause of an unfinished Indian revolution and especially of an unfinished peasant revolution. But it does not recognise any responsibility for its own failure to overcome people's passivity and raise their level of consciousness and organisation. Such non-responsible orientation is basically at variance with the spirit of Marxism. It is only by recognising one's own responsibility that

Indian Marxism can make a break from fatalism and recapture its revolutionary quality.

One of the greatest theoretical stumbling blocks in the way of a forward movement is the equation of Marxism with *economic determinism*. The view that for peasant emancipation a change in the economic basis is the basic condition ignores the role of the human forces themselves in effecting a change in this basis. How to generate these forces is the most important problem facing Indian Marxism. India has perhaps had one of the most exploited and oppressed peasantry in the world. The Indian peasant has also been subject to the worst forms of social degradation as reflected in caste and untouchability. And yet the response of the Indian peasantry to this situation has been characterised by passivity with occasional outbreaks of peasant rebellion. This fatalistic attitude of the peasant, reflected in non-responsibility for his own fate, is the hardest problem at the root of which lie centuries of cultural backwardness and perverse social conditioning of the peasantry.

It must also be stated that if passivity represents one form of this non-responsibility for one's fate, the rebelliousness or the leaning towards primitive anarchism, which is now becoming a common feature in India, is another form of the denial of the principle of responsibility. Whether fatalism assumes a passive or an aggressive, naked or a disguised form, fatalism is fatalism. And it must be recognised as such before a break can be made from it.

In my opinion the greatest contribution made by Marx was in drawing attention to fatalism as the hard core of the Indian problem in his articles on India. His theoretical contribution lay in pointing to the social roots of this fatalism. In a classical portrayal of peasant passivity, Marx observed how the peasantry "concentrating on some miserable patch of land, had quietly witnessed the ruin of empires, the perpetration of unspeakable cruelties, the massacre of the population of large towns, with no other consideration bestowed upon them than on natural events"; how the *village system* "subjected man to external circumstances instead of elevating man to be the sovereign of circumstances"; and how the peasantry was "deprived of all grandeur and historical energies." (Karl Marx, 1955, pp. 36-37). Marx thought that by undermining the village system (or the objective basis of peasant passivity) British rule had "produced the greatest, and to speak the truth, the only social *revolution* in Asia" (Ibid.). In other words, Marx suggested that British rule had created the objective conditions of peasant emancipation from the social outlook of fatalism. But what about the *subjective* conditions of the release from fatalism?

Indian Marxists never understood the full significance of this true legacy of Marx for India, indeed for the whole of Asia. They have still to pick up the thread from where Marx left it and have to reformulate both the objective and the subjective conditions of a non-fatalistic outlook. Faith in the supernatural and superhuman powers resulting in passivity, faithlessness resulting in primitive rebelliousness—here lies the quintessence of a fatalistic outlook. A break from faith as well as faithlessness, the development of a critical self-consciousness and a positive assumption of responsibility for one's own fate—this is what is the meaning of a break from fatalism. This is also the beginning of a truly modern consciousness. In trying to create this non-fatalistic consciousness, Indian Marxists would find in Gandhi's thought and practice their strongest ally; they would also find in Gandhi their strongest philosophical adversary. They would meet with tough resistance from their own theoretical orientations of the earlier period. But in the very process of grappling with the problem of a new consciousness under changed conditions of existence, Gandhism (which represented the semi-conscious state of half-awake peasantry) and Indian Marxism (which represented, and continues to represent, the primitive rebelliousness or the economism of the half-peasant, half-worker of the Indian scene)—both would be superseded.

It should be appreciated that both Marxism and Gandhism have their roots in the common problem of human alienation. Gandhism was the product of the historical encounter between the forces of defensive, pre-industrial and pre-capitalist Asian civilisation and those of an aggressive, industrial-capitalist civilisation. Marxism, on the other hand, was the product of new social forces within industrialism itself which looked beyond capitalism. Marxism embodies the struggle for a new social structure making man the sovereign and not the slave of the productive forces generated through his efforts. The basic question posed by Gandhism concerning the fate of the small producer and the artisan and of the pre-industrial society in the modern age can be taken over only by Marxism which simultaneously looks beyond both pre-capitalism and capitalism.

In countries like India the worker and the peasant are linked through indissoluble bonds insofar as the worker of today is yesterday's peasant who has not yet fully broken his umbilical cord with the village. The problem of peasant consciousness and organisation cannot be solved without bringing the scattered peasant much closer to the organised worker. Similarly, the problem of retrieving the worker from the blind alley of crude economism or anarchism cannot be solved without making the worker conscious of his obligations to an insecurity-and-poverty-stricken peasantry. The concept of hegemony is thus, realised through the *worker-peasant alliance* which is the culmination and embodiment of an integrated social consciousness. This alliance would remove the continuing hiatus between Gandhism and Indian Marxism.

Marxism representing this integrated and higher form of consciousness would have no resemblance with its primitive form with which we have been familiar in the past. By grappling at the highest theoretical and abstract levels with the concrete problems thrown up by the practical-political movement, and by linking up the creation of theory with direct and active interaction with the people and their problems, Marxism would throw up a new type of intellectual capable of acting as a force of Indian cultural and political renewal. We began this essay with a quotation from Gramsci emphasising the inner contradictions and tensions within Marxism itself through which the revolutionary potentialities of Marxism are realised. We conclude this essay with another quotation from Gramsci which shows the process of creation of a new type of intelligentsia:

"In any case one could only have had cultural stability and an organic quality of thought if there had existed the same unity between the intellectuals and the simple as there should be between theory and practice. That is, if the intellectuals had been organically the intellectuals of those masses, and if they had worked out and made coherent the principles and the problems raised by the masses in their practical activity, thus constituting a cultural and social bloc. The question posed here was the one we have already referred to, namely, this: is a philosophical movement properly so called when it is devoted to creating a specialised culture among restricted intellectual groups, or rather when, and only when, in the process of elaborating a form of thought superior to "common sense" and coherent on a scientific plane, it never forgets to remain in contact with the "simple" and indeed finds in this contact the source of the problems it sets out to study and resolve? Only by this contact does a philosophy become historical, purify itself of intellectualistic elements of an individual character and become 'life'. (Gramsci, 1971, p. 330).

Notes and References

1. It is important to note that Marxism which was the product of an industrial society underwent qualitative change when it was transplanted into societies which were not yet industrially developed. In Russia Marxism turned into Stalinism and in China into Maoism. Some aspects of Stalinism represented a gross vulgarisation of Marxism, a break from the rational and humanist tradition of Marxism. This internal metamorphosis of Marxism brings out the significance of interaction between forms of consciousness and conditions of social existence. If Marxist theory is a force for bringing about a change in conditions of social existence, it is also necessary that conditions of social existence should in certain respects be ripe and favourable for receiving Marxist theory. Pre-industrial (and pre-capitalist) conditions of social existence, therefore, force a distortion in the theoretical consciousness itself as shown by the examples of Stalinism and also to some extent by Maoism.

2. Gramsci suggests how the fatalistic orientation is a phase in the evolution of Marxist thought and practice in many countries. It is even a source of self-assurance and cohesion of the political groups at a lower level of consciousness. To quote Gramsci, "fatalism is nothing other than the clothing worn by real and active will when in a weak position" (1971, p. 337).
3. To quote Marx: "Ignorance is a demon and we are afraid it will play more than one tragedy; the greatest Greek poets were right when they represented it in the terrible drama of the royal house of Mycenae and Thebes as tragic fate." (Karl Marx, 1957, p. 39).
4. E.M.S. Namboodiripad has taken sharp exception to the use of the term "pamphlet Marxism". He feels that I am making fun of Indian Marxists as those who indulge themselves in 'pamphlet Marxism' (E.M.S. Namboodiripad, 1974, p. 59). My intention, however, was not to make fun of either the courageous group of early propagators of Marxism in India or of the tendency to write Marxist pamphlets. Pamphlet Marxism was used by me as a capsule term for attempts at simplifying Marxism in a manner leading to fundamental revision of Marx's basic ideas. It is for this reason that Engels in his well-known letter to Bloc recommended the study of Marx's theory 'from its original sources and not at second hand' (Karl Marx, 1964, p. 18).
5. A critical review expressing similar ideas has been offered in recent years by Asok Sen (1969, pp. 158-82) and Baudhayan Chatopadhyaya (1969, pp. 205-60). Also see the recent attempts at re-evaluation of the Bengal renaissance (V.C. Joshi, 1975).
6. Commenting on this, Gramsci observes: "... in the most recent development of the philosophy of praxis the exploration and refinement of the concept of the unity of theory and practice is still only at an early stage. There still remain residues of mechanicism since people speak about theory as 'complement' or an 'accessory' or the handmaid of practice. It would seem right for this question too to be considered historically as an aspect of the political question of the intellectuals." (1971, p. 334).

    In a footnote Gramsci further elaborates this point: "The notion of the subservience of theory to practice ... has been widespread in the Marxist movement, in forms as diverse as Stalin's formulation 'theory must serve practice' (Works, Vol. VI, p. 88) and Rosa Luxemberg's argument... that 'theory only develops to the extent that the need for it is created by the practice of the movement." (Gramsci, 1971, p. 334, fn. 17).

Books Referred to in the Text

1. Baudhayan Chattopadhaya, 'India's Economic Crisis', in P.C. Joshi (ed.), *Homage to Marx*, New Delhi, 1969.
2. F. Engels, *The Peasant War in Germany*, Moscow, 1956.
3. Antonio Gramsci, *The Modern Prince and Other Essays*, New York, 1957.
4. Antonio Gramsci, *Selections from the Prison Notebooks*, New York, 1971.
5. V.C. Joshi (ed.), *Rammohun Roy and the Process of Modernisation in India*, New Delhi, 1975.
6. Simon Kuznets, *Economic Growth and Structure*, New Delhi, 1965.
7. V.I. Lenin, *Collected Works*, Vol. 5, Moscow, 1961.
8. Karl Marx, *A Contribution to the Critique of Political Economy*, Moscow, 1970.
9. Karl Marx and F. Engels, *On Religion*, Moscow, 1957.
10. Karl Marx and F. Engels, *Selected Works*, Vol. I, Bombay, 1955.
11. Karl Marx, *On Colonialism*, Moscow, 1955.
12. Karl Marx, *Capital*, Vol. I, New Delhi, 1955.
13. Karl Marx, *Economic and Philosophical Manuscripts of 1844*, Moscow.
14. E.M.S. Namboodiripad, *How I Became A Communist*, Trivandrum, 1976.
15. E.M.S. Namboodiripad, 'How to Study Indian Communism with Minimum Reading', *Social Scientist*, No. 25, August 1974.
16. E.M.S. Namboodiripad, *Economics and Politics of India's Socialist Pattern*, New Delhi, 1966.
17. Ajit Roy, 'Marxism and India', *Social Scientist*, No. 26, September 1974.
18. Asok Sen, 'The Petty-Bourgeois Default', in P.C. Joshi (ed.), *Homage to Marx*, New Delhi, 1969.
19. Mao Tse-tung, *Selected Works*, Vol. II, Bombay, 1954.
20. Mao Tse-tung, *Selected Works*, Vol. III, Bombay, 1954.

2

Roots of the Politico-Economic Problem: Basis-Superstructure Relations Reconsidered

It is the problem of the relations between structure and superstructure which must be accurately posed and resolved if the forces which are active in the history of a particular period are to be correctly analysed and the relations between them determined. Two principles must orient the discussion:1. That no society sets itself tasks for whose accomplishment the necessary and sufficient conditions do not either already exist or are at least now beginning to emerge and develop;[2] that no society breaks down and can be replaced till it has first developed all the forms of life which are implicit in its internal relations. From a reflection on those two principles, one can move on to develop a whole series of further principles of historical methodology. Meanwhile, in studying a structure, it is necessary to distinguish organic movements (relatively permanent) from movements which may be termed 'conjunctural' (and which appear as occasional, immediate, and almost accidental)....

The dialectical connection between the two categories of movements and therefore research, is hard to establish precisely. Moreover, if error is serious in historiography, it becomes still more serious in the art of politics, when it is not reconstruction of past history but the construction of present and future history which is at stake. One's own baser and more immediate desires and passions are the cause of error, in that they take the place of an objective and impartial analysis and this happens not as a conscious 'means' to stimulate to action, but as self-deception. In this case too the snake bites the snake-charmer—in other words the demagogue is the first victim of his own demagogy.

— Antonio Gramsci, *Prison Notebooks*, pp. 177-79.

Perhaps no particular year since India's independence has brought into sharp focus all the underlying contradictions of the Indian politico-economic system as the outgoing year. 1973 has been a year of crisis which has put a fundamental re-appraisal of this system on the agenda.

The interpretations of the nature of the present crisis appear broadly to follow two different lines. According to one interpretation the basic health of the system is sound. The crisis is, therefore, a transitory phenomenon caused mainly by accidental factors. Conditions are in due course expected to return to normalcy as crisis-generating factors (e.g. the draught) cease to operate and crisis-resolving factors (e.g. good weather) take their place. An implicit assumption of this view is the faith in the self-correcting powers of the system and a lack of insistence on comprehensive social intervention. Even those who do not believe in the efficacy of the self-correcting mechanism, however, favour not any major intervention from outside. In fact, many believe that too much (or wrong) intervention (through excessive controls), licensing policy, nationalisation and curbs on private enterprise has itself caused the crisis. They recommend, therefore, only such action as would restore the normal functioning of the system. It is expected that the return to 'normalcy' would solve the most pressing problems. Even when they refrain from boldly asserting such a point of view, influential sections of the ruling elite also subscribe to it.

The second interpretation tends to locate the source of the crisis within the system rather than outside it. Therefore, it looks for a way out of the crisis not in any tinkering but in a total overhaul of the system. It views the crisis as a process of disintegration of the system or as a generator of social forces destined to cause a breakdown of the system. Some holding this point of view have a kind of fatalistic faith in spontaneity or in the operation of self-destroying contradictions within the system. They are, therefore, convinced of the futility of any "constructive" initiative to save the system. Many others in this group, however, are deeply suspicious of any "constructive" measures undertaken with a view to softening the crisis and stabilising the system. If at all any conscious intervention is desired, it is of a type that aggravates the crisis of the system and accelerates the process of its disintegration. But even these critics have adopted the less arduous alternative of verbal exposure of the bankruptcy of the system than of social mobilisation to change it. In practice, therefore, even the latter variety of critics are believers in the inevitable doom of the system through the operation of natural processes.

It is a curious paradox of recent history that two widely divergent, indeed opposite, ideologies, one 'reformist' and another 'revolutionary', have converged on one fundamental point; a worship of spontaneity and a lack of insistence on conscious social action. The reformists and revolutionaries are both turning into passive spectators of events insofar as they have succumbed to the paralysing influence of the myths and rationalisations they themselves have created. They even fail to grasp the obvious that neither the possibilities of the system (the conception of the ruling elite) nor its limits (the view of the critics) can be demonstrated except in the process of making the system work.

For changing the system it is not enough for a critical minority to perceive on the basis of its intuition or its scientific knowledge that the system has constraints. It is the common people, whose verdict finally counts, who have to be led towards the realisation of the constraints of the system through their own experience. And there is no other way of carrying conviction to them except by fully and genuinely exhausting the possibilities of the system. Indeed there are no shortcuts to a social revolution. Isn't it one of the fundamentals of the science of revolution that no social system breaks down and can be replaced till it has first developed and exhausted all its productive potentialities? It is also one of the lessons of history that "men make their history but they do not make it as they please; they do not make it under circumstances chosen by themselves but under circumstances directly encountered, given and transmitted from the past".

And here both the supporters and the critics of the system need to ask themselves how far they have really tried to explore the possibilities and limits of the system in terms specially of the needs and aspirations of the underprivileged classes. And it should be said very bluntly that this is a task not for demagogues, dilettantes and lazy-bones; it calls for combining a high level of dedication with expertise; a firm adherence to principles with the ability to opertionalise them or to fight them out at the level of details. Such a task makes unprecedented demands on society's innovative and organising ability and, above all, on its commitment to the scientific method.

One has to give a high weightage to the scientific approach because the potential or the lack of potential of a system are strictly empirical questions. They can be resolved only by a rigorously scientific enquiry into concrete realities and not by reliance only on the inner voice of charismatic leaders or the arbitrary judgements of party bosses and functionaries. It should not be forgotten that societies which gave greater weight to sorcery rather than to science paid a very high price. For, the surrender to arbitrariness in decision-making resulted in restricting the range of choices and, therefore, in imposing harsher burdens on the people than were warranted by circumstances.

Considered from an objective standpoint, neither the classical capitalist nor the classical socialist pattern should serve as the ideals to be followed by the Third World countries like India today. If classical capitalism assumed the form of an elemental upheaval where man was the object rather than the subject of history, classical socialism especially under Stalin did not represent the full flowering of the idea of development as a conscious social process. For, here the will of an arbitrary leader rather than the widest human initiative became the prime mover of social development. History shows that backwardness inflicted its own penalties specially on those who were the first to rebel against it. The war against backwardness had to be fought out by the pioneers within the constraints created by backwardness itself.

In this background India's choice to achieve development with social justice within a democratic framework is an audacious exercise without precedent in history. And this choice to find a humane solution to the economic problem has not yet been matched by an understanding of the full implications of this choice and the obligations that it involves for all classes of Indian society. In this context the question arises whether India's choice of the system is adequate considering the choice of her ambitious goals? Does India show promise of any success in this venture? Or would she be forced ultimately to regress into an Indian variant of any of the past patterns rather than throw up a new one?

All these questions require a consistently scientific approach and harmful consequences follow in the absence of it. For instance, in formulating criteria for assessing economic systems or for suggesting changes in them a short-cut is sometimes adopted. There is no thorough examination of the performance of a particular system with reference to the needs of various classes or to what a change in it would imply for them in the concrete conditions of a particular country. The very fact that certain ideological and institutional forms were the concomitants of the capitalist or socialist transition in developed countries seems enough to justify their adoption or choice by a developing country. In other words, there is a confusion between goals and the means of achieving these goals.

It must be stated very categorically that certain features which were associated with classical socialism were not the result of voluntary choice. Special mention should be made here of the forcible elimination of the capitalist sector and of the peasant economy or the conversion of the "dictatorship of the proletariat" into a regime of naked terror and suppression of dissent. In fact, Russia under Lenin was eager to achieve the economic transition to socialism with the least disruption of the productive apparatus and with minimum resort to coercion against its own class base and allies. It was, however, forced to adopt confiscatory and coercive measures under political compulsions beyond its control. To consider them, therefore, to be essential aspects of the socialist transition for all countries regardless of their needs and conditions is to permit colossal destruction of material resources and human skills, economic dislocation and social suffering which the backward countries can ill afford.

Such imitative rather than a creative approach to the institutional problems of development has had disastrous consequences in many East European and Third World countries. Above all, it has blurred the cognition of new opportunities. In the past, as in Russia, drastic economic solutions had to be resorted to as a means of solving the political problems. Today it may perhaps be possible to find political solutions to many economic problems. In other words, *by strengthening the political safeguards would it not be possible today to use the capitalist sector in the national interest to a far greater extent than was possible under the classical socialist pattern?* Such a policy, however, can be implemented only by a leadership whose political incorruptibility and commitment to the new society are beyond question, which has the solid support of a strong mass movement, and which is determined to deal ruthlessly with the problem of conspicuous consumption, political corruption and subversion of national goals and priorities by moneyed interests. It also presupposes a certain responsiveness of at least important sections of the capitalists to the national tasks.

And yet past experience shows that there is no escape from trying out this alternative. For, if the forces of capitalism are locked up and not consciously directed into desirable productive channels, they pose a bigger threat by turning collaborationist, or by seeking outlets in conspicuous consumption and mercantile and usurious modes of exploitation. Moreover, the deliberate exclusion of the capitalist sector out of the process of national resource mobilisation further perpetuates dependence on foreign sources, thus putting national independence itself into jeopardy. Finally, the peaceful road to social change in India would be a mirage if no distinction is made between the productive and the unproductive sections of the bourgeoisie.

Another difficulty in properly using the potentialities of the system emanates from the tendency to treat it as something fixed or the path of its evolution as predetermined. In this way the constraints of the system are exaggerated. It is overlooked that the system is what you make of it, that it is an evolving one. One should constantly keep in view its inner contradictions which offer possibilities of changing it. The system is on the one hand, a set of normative principles constituting the unifying framework of a multi-class national movement. It is also, on the other hand, a set of institutions which have crystallised during a given period on the basis of a definite balance of class forces. While the normative principles have a definite bias for the deprived and oppressed classes, the institutional forms as evolved since independence have a bias against them on account of their organisational weaknesses.

It has always been the tendency of the privileged classes to treat these institutional forms within which they are privileged as the essence of the system; they pay only lip-service to the normative principles. But the profound emotional appeal and the tremendous mobilising power of normative principles should not be ignored as is so often done by the spokesmen of the dominant classes as well as by those who claim to represent the weaker sections. Indeed, for these weaker sections the normative principles rather than the institutional forms are the core of the system; these principles legitimise their struggle for a change from the old to new institutional forms.

In agrarian societies like India, still suffering from the socio-economic ravages of colonial rule, the weaker sections like peasants, artisans and labourers are not a minority; indeed they constitute almost the whole society. *And for these poverty-stricken millions the normative principles and the given institutional forms pull in opposite directions; the former affirm social justice and the latter negate it. This inner contradiction of the present system has sooner or later to be resolved; there is no escape from it.* It is, however, a stupendous task calling for the demolition of age-old structures and creation of new ones to replace them.

A basic weakness of reformers and revolutionaries in many Asian countries is that they are more negative than positive in their approach. They often advocate or try the demolition of the old without also providing the substitute for it. But the effects of such a one-sided change for the vast millions living below subsistence levels in agrarian societies are disastrous. It takes away the element of security in the old system and lands them into greater insecurity. In more concrete terms, it is beyond dispute that there can be no economic growth or social justice for the rural masses so long as parasitic landlordism and the deadening grips of the usurer and the trader are not eliminated. Land reforms, social control of rural credit and trade in agricultural commodities are, therefore, necessary to resolve the tension between the normative principles and the exploitative economic order ruling in the countryside. This is, however, only one part of the story.

The other part is that landlordism, usury and trade are not just exploitative. Under given conditions they also provide to the masses an economic basis for their subsistence. The landlords, usurers and traders are exploiters all right. But they also provide land and consumption loans to the poor who have little or no resources of their own and suffer from a deficit all round the year. Any disturbance in this system without providing a substitute, therefore, brings incalculable harm to the masses. It is for this reason that the peasant is both eager for and fearful of change. He is willing to try out radicals and reformers, but if they are found wanting, he is not unwilling to put his faith in conservative regimes in search of security. Ineffective reforms and the insecurity caused by them have, therefore, led to traditionalist backlash in many countries.

To say all this is not to plead for maintaining the status quo but only to distinguish between a merely romantic and genuinely revolutionary approach to the question of social change. It is also to emphasise that in planning for rural change the negative and the positive steps should go together. And the process of destroying the old should at a given time be carried only to the point warranted by the organisational capacity for constructing the new. It should not be overlooked that even small advances in the positive direction are not easy to achieve in the rural sector without enormous organisational work at the grassroots. And this requires millions of social workers who combine dedication and expertise with a sense of realities.

Such a positive approach has been alien to those talking the loudest about the rural masses. For an understanding of the problems of changing the present institutional forms or for success in grappling with them it is necessary to go beyond empty radicalism; so common among urban politicians and intellectuals. What is needed is a direct contact with the realities as they are. The important thing that such contact reveals is that the *need for change or the desire for it* do not automatically produce the *capacity for it*. The latter has to be created through sustained effort at ground level to raise the level of social consciousness and organisation. And there is no short cut to this effort. The growth of social consciousness and organisation is again a positive task. Why is it that there has been no success in India in this direction? Certain factors thwarting this growth can be indicated. There is, firstly, the factor of urban bias or urban dominance in the economic, political and cultural sphere. The old habit of treating the rural sector as a hinterland of the urban centres has not yet entirely disappeared. This leads to far greater weightage to a few urban centres in the planning process than to the villages. There is also the regular brain drain from the rural to the urban areas. Consequently, the process of new leadership formation has lagged far behind the disintegration of the old leadership structure. It is not the rural masses alone which are faced with a leadership vacuum; it is the rural society as a whole which suffers from a crisis of leadership.

What has further aggravated this vacuum is the absence of a creative approach from outside. For if it is agreed that the rural society is incapable of generating the forces of transformation from within itself, the role of intervention or lack of intervention from outside becomes truly decisive. But a positive intervention from outside has not been forthcoming in recent years. No section of the Indian elite has even tried to pose the question of concretising the normative principles thrown up by the national movement into definite cultural and institutional patterns appropriate to the present stage of Indian society. Surrender to spontaneity has by and large characterised the approach of leading groups to this vital question, further reinforcing, consequently, the leadership vacuum.

One must first mention the die-hard conservatives who are the worst defaulters. They do not recognise the need or importance of such an effort; they even block any effort in this direction. They refuse to see that the disintegration of the old society has reached such an advanced stage that it cannot be held together either by the old normative principles or by the cultural and institutional patterns in which those principles were embodied. The old social order is in shambles; it cannot be brought back to life. What is not clearly perceived by the ideologists of the old order is, however, perceived without any difficulty by the dominant classes of the old society. And in their struggle for survival they recognise and seek desperately to preserve as much as possible of the privileges which they enjoyed in the old order; but they tend to disregard their obligations. This factor has contributed the most towards eroding the value-basis or the legitimacy of the old order.

For, no social order can be viable if the dominant classes only cling to their privileges without accepting the obligations which accompanied them. A class continues to be a leading class only so long as it is also aware of its obligations to other classes. If its attitude towards other classes becomes divorced from a normative basis and is guided purely by expediency, or if the norm itself becomes one of using whatever is useful for the narrow advantage of an individual or a class, the inner integrating principles of social existence break down. The problem of new integrative principles or a new normative basis of social existence then becomes the foremost need of society. There also becomes prominent then the role of a social class capable of filling up the social vacuum and fulfilling this need. But the appearance of this inner need and the rise of a social class capable of fulfilling this need are not simultaneous processes. A long period may intervene between the two processes, a period of trial and error, of suffering and ordeal, of experimentation and failure.

The conservative forces may try to conceal the real nature of this crisis by calling it a collapse of "law and order". They may even try to impose an authoritarian regime in the name of restoring law and order. But this is no more than a false answer to a real problem. In ancient countries like India which had to undergo also the experience of distorted social evolution due to colonial rule, the birth pangs of a new social order are bound to be prolonged and pervasive. What makes this process more poignant is the lack of appreciation of this problem so common among the Indian elite.

Apart from the die-hard conservatives, there are also the ultra-radicals who suffer from a different kind of intellectual constraint. They locate the source of this crisis in the very existence of a class system and are of the view that it can be solved only by eliminating the class system itself. That this view is fundamentally sound cannot be disputed. The error lies in having primitive-anarchistic views of classes and class conflicts. One such view is that in the very process of destroying the class system or overthrowing the dominant classes the new society would be born. This outlook has sometimes taken the very crude shape of killing the leading members of the old ruling class as symbolic of the destruction of the old order and the emergence of a new order. No intellectual critique of this view is required to prove its bankruptcy. In modern times it has nowhere succeeded in destroying the old order; in fact, such a policy has led to fascist counter-terror by vested interests to defend the old order. Primitive rebels have a certain tragic grandeur associated with them in past history. But in the contemporary period the re-enactment of this drama by elements from the Westernised intelligentsia is more infantile than tragic.

The more difficult to detect and to eradicate are, however, the less crude and the more subtle forms of anarchism or opportunism which characterise the approach of respectable political parties and other social groups. And here the socio-economic deprivation and injustice to which the lower classes are subjected in a class society lends legitimacy to the pressures for eliminating them and for mobilising the lower classes against their exploiters and oppressors. The struggle between classes may assume the form of simple "economism" which is aimed at improving the economic position of the havenots within the system. The aim here is to ensure for the havenots a larger share of the national cake by strengthening their bargaining power. Alternatively, the political rather than the economic aspect may be assigned primacy in class conflict. Thus it may assume the form of movements for capture of power in the interest of the havenots whether through peaceful or non-peaceful means, whether through the use of guns or the ballot box. In India political parties claiming to represent the havenots have tried to channelise class conflict along the lines of crude economism as well as capture of political power.

The inadequacy of these approaches to the class problem is revealed by the poor results that have been achieved. Even in terms of the economic aim of improving the position of the havenots, crude economism has been only a partial success, if not a failure, because it does not touch the very roots of the economic weakness of the lower classes. For, in an economically and socially backward country the problem of increasing the share of the havenots in the national product cannot be divorced from a policy of ensuring a sustained increase in the national product itself. Moreover, in the peculiar situation of under-development in countries like India the poor are not synonymous with the wage earners. In fact, in the case of the vast sections of the poor, including specially the rural poor, poverty is perpetuated because the poor are outside those main forms of economic activity where the major part of the national product is generated. They are outside the organised sector where redistribution of the product in favour of the poor can be brought about through various known forms of economism, i.e. trade union action aimed at strengthening the bargaining power of the wage earners. Economics in the Indian setting leaves almost untouched the vast poverty-stricken masses which are in the unorganised sector; it has, therefore, very little anti-poverty potential. An anti-poverty programme here has to be innovative; it has to provide the poor a stake in the economic system or an opportunity for livelihood.

The problem of the vast masses of small producers and labourers having no regular employment thus cannot be tackled by the classical type of economism. They are marginal groups in the present economic system. But constituting the majority in agrarian societies, they represent unutilised economic potential of vast magnitude. Their problem calls for more positive thinking and action at several levels which go beyond conventional economism.

This brings us to the political role of economism. In fact, economism today not only perpetuates the deprivation of the unprivileged. It has overstimulated the economic appetites of those already better-off, thus alienating them totally from the truly "wretched of the earth". What sustains economism as a resilient force is its tie-up with politics as it operates today. Economism thrives because it serves as a short-cut to political power. And it has a mobilising potential in the manipulative power-struggle as it goes on in the present political climate. Economism as a political technique has thus led to the conversion of regular wage-earners and salaried classes at all levels into powerful pressure groups led by politicians and trade unionists functioning as skilled manipulators and intermediaries between employers (i.e. the government or the private sector magnates) and the employees. And this whole game of manipulating the power structure and the distribution of gains of development in favour of only a section of society to the point of total neglect of the genuine havenots goes on in the name of carrying forward the class struggle. Seldom was perhaps such a mundane and vulgar game carried on in the name of a great cause as in India during the last twenty-five years.

This game is a cause for concern not only because of its indifference to those who are too weak, fragmented and disorganised to play this game. It is a greater cause for alarm because of its unconcern towards the growth of productive forces and its contribution to the economic stagnation in India today.

The surrender of organised labour to such crude and short-sighted economism has led many to pose the question *whether in underdeveloped countries like India the Marxist view of the role of the working class having nothing to lose but its chains is at all relevant; whether it is a force for social change or for social status quo. It is also pertinent to ask whether the present leaders of organised labour—or the champions of economism —can at all be regarded as revolutionary*. It should be remembered that only that political force can be called genuinely revolutionary which is linked with most deprived strata of society; and which is struggling all the time to mobilise all the other classes of society to the needs and aspirations of the deprived strata. From this standpoint a genuinely revolutionary political force is still to emerge in India.

In Gandhi we had the rudimentary expression of such a political force. But it did not last beyond Gandhi. Gandhi's contribution lay in mobilising the support of the unorganised sector for Indian nationalism and making it aware of the existence of the dumb, half-starving millions belonging to this section. The normative principles bequeathed by Gandhi to Indian nationalism derive their importance from their commitment to the cause of these millions, Gandhi's *Daridranarayan*. But all major questions pertaining to the nature of the institutional framework or pattern of development required for the uplift of these millions have yet to be squarely posed and resolved by the Indian elite. These have by and large been evaded since independence.

To resume the main thread of our argument, the reduction of class conflict into economism has in the past benefited mainly the organised strata rather than the vast unorganised masses. Even when class conflict has assumed the political form of struggle for power, it has not improved the fortunes or the prospects of these unorganised masses. When this struggle has been conducted through the non-parliamentary means in certain pockets of the country, the political groups engaged in this struggle have failed to win over or mobilise these masses for any action programme. The heroic actions of the vanguard have by and large been substituted for the painstaking tasks of educating, organising and activising the masses. "A heroic minority and the passive majority", this sums up the importance of this variety of non-parliamentary road to power. This road has not resulted anywhere in India in the capture of power by the political groups who claim to represent the masses. It invariably leaves the masses in a blind alley.

Take now the parliamentary road to political power. Since it is based on adult franchise and, therefore, on capturing the votes of large numbers of people, parliamentarism has a double face. It is outwardly committed to *populism*, or to arousing the expectations of the people in general. *But fundamentally it is based on manipulation rather than mobilisation.* Power in the narrow interest of a privileged minority is cleverly disguised here as the pursuit of power in the general interest of the majority. As parliamentary politics becomes manipulative politics, it becomes legitimate to use any and all means so long as they serve the purpose of capturing the votes of the majority. Parliamentary politics thus gets linked with money power, on the one hand, and opportunism or lack of principle, on the other. As a result, parliamentary politics fails to become the politics of the unorganised masses *for* them and *by* them. Their lack of money power or lack of access to money power prevents them from acting in defiance of those who control money power.

What is worse is that the social and cultural backwardness of the masses is exploited by vested interests to secure their electoral support. Thus religion, caste, regionalism and various other elements of medievalist obscurantism are actively mobilised to keep the masses divided among themselves and to incapacitate them from emerging as a united political force. Parliamentary politics thus reduces itself into a form of politics under which the unenlightened masses allow themselves to be mobilised against their own genuine interests. Far from acting as an instrument of mass emancipation, it has acted as a force for perpetuating the backwardness of the masses.

The more parliamentary politics gets divorced from any positive principle or from the genuine interests of the masses, or in other words, the more it degenerates into opportunism, the more it leads towards strengthening the various tendencies of anarchism. Opportunism and anarchism thus merge as two sides of the same coin. They go on reinforcing each other, thus creating a vicious circle. Both opportunism and anarchism, however, lead only to an impasse.

We have earlier mentioned the more aggressive and naked form of anarchism. But mention must also be made of a less belligerent form of anarchism which has, from the point of view of social change, turned out to be as ineffectual a philosophy or strategy as other forms of anarchism or liberalism. We are referring here to the *Sarvodaya* ideology which is also anarchistic in the fundamental philosophical sense. If overt anarchism adopts an adventurist strategy for capture of political power, covert anarchism tries to solve the problems of rural masses without reference to the question of State authority or power. It is committed to anti-Statism or non-State form of intervention in economic and social affairs. In the name of emancipating society from the tyranny of the State, it seeks to mobilise a band of dedicated social workers for the service of the weakest sections of society without reference to the State. This ostrich-like policy of wishing away the existence of the State only means that the State is left to be managed and manipulated by the privileged classes. Moreover, the masses are thus deprived of the possibility of using the most powerful instrument of action, viz. the State for their own advancement. Such anti-state or non-state ideologies, which arise on the basis of the popular revulsion against abuse or misuse of power, are thus as ineffectual from the social point of view as are ideologies sanctifying the pursuit of power without social purpose.

The *power-crazy politician* and the *power-shunning social worker* are, from the point of view of subjective motivation, poles apart. The former typifies self-aggrandisement and the latter self-effacement. In the former one finds the sharpest reflection of the baser side of human nature and in the latter its nobler side. But judged objectively from the point of the requirement of social movement, the two are not fundamentally different. Both arise on the basis of the apathy and passivity of the masses and both tend to perpetuate this backwardness and passivity.

Indeed there are heroes and heroes in history. There are heroes whose heroism is the other side of the unheroism of the masses; and there are others who emerge as heroes in the process of raising the masses to a heroic stature. In India after independence we have had only heroes of the former kind rather than of the latter. In this sense the period since independence has been a most unheroic age; for it has by and large evaded the question of breaking the apathy and the passivity of the masses. And the consequences of this default should be very clearly recognised. An elite which does not address itself to the challenge of breaking the passivity of its people destroys the sources of its own energy and creativity; it degenerates into an irresponsible power group combining parasitism with deceit or tyranny. Political irresponsibility, authoritarianism and social parasitism of the elite are in the ultimate sense a reflection of the passive resignation of the masses, the attitude so aptly captured in the line from poet Tulsidas: *Kou Nrip Hoe Hamen Ka Hani* (whoever is the ruler, how does it concern us?). In other words, a dynamic elite can emerge only in the process of trying to transform the passive masses into an active force.

Why has such passivity of the masses continued despite important changes in India since independence? What are the roots of this passivity and what can be done to deal with this problem? To ask these questions is to deal with one of the most unexplored dimensions of Indian social history, viz. the distortions in the relationship between the basis and superstructure of Indian society introduced by British rule and later continued even after independence. Space does not permit us to explore this problem in great depth. We pose only some issues to stimulate further discussion.

British rule made certain drastic changes both at the level of the basis and the superstructure; but the changes made at the level of the superstructure were far more drastic than at the level of the basis. These changes in the superstructure had no correspondence with the compulsions and needs of the basis of the native society. They were motivated by the requirements of preserving and perpetuating India's colonial status; they were required by the compulsions and needs of the society of the Imperial country. In countries like India which were under the direct occupation of imperialism, the inroads into the superstructure were far more drastic and thorough-going than in those countries (e.g. China) which were subject to indirect colonialism. In particular, the imperialist cultural penetration was far more pervasive and pernicious under conditions of direct domination than under those of indirect domination.

On no other question since independence has the surrender to spontaneity been more pronounced and gone unchallenged as on the question of a change in the superstructure. For, here the Marxists as well as the non-Marxists have been incapacitated from any conscious intervention by the widely shared assumption that the change in the superstructure would follow automatically as a consequence of change in the economic basis of society. Within the superstructure, if there was any sphere where a positive policy was most urgently needed as a corrective to the corrosive influence of the colonial rule, it was the cultural sphere. And it was this sphere which was almost entirely left to the forces of spontaneity. The consequences of this policy, or the lack of cultural policy, were very serious. Here lies the key to an understanding of the continuing passivity of the masses.

Earlier we noted that in *India today there is a wide gap between the need for change and the desire for it, on the one hand, and the capacity for effecting this change, on the other.* This capacity for change is another name for the release of creative initiative and energy of the people. And this release of initiative and energy always presupposes a cultural renewal of the people as a whole. Here lies the basic difference between the adjustment process of animals and of human beings to changing conditions. While animals passively adapt themselves to the environment, human beings have the potentiality to actively change their natural and social environments in accordance with their needs and aspirations. And as Marx said, *the most enterprising animals are inferior to the least enterprising men insofar as the latter first create the plan of their action in their imagination; before a change is actually accomplished in practice*, they have first a certain conception or a vision of this change which emancipates them from the fear of the unknown and which mobilises them for collective action. Since action is social action and practice is social practice these are by and large dependent on the emergence of a *new* idea, a *new* concept, a *new* ideal which are capable of capturing the imagination of the people and investing their action with a new meaning.

Judged from the above angle, the passivity of the people only implies a breakdown of the old intellectual framework, the meaning of the system and the value-frame which was the motivating force for collective action within the context of social conditions existing in the past. It means that a change in these social conditions has led to the obsolescence of the old moral and intellectual basis of social existence. The passivity of the masses, therefore, cannot be broken without positively grappling with this problem of *cultural vacuum* arising as a result of the breakdown of the old values and norms and the lack of growth of new values and norms.

It needs to be emphasised that the cultural vacuum only means the lack of a cultural basis for *conscious* social action. It does not mean that there is no social action. What it implies is that social action is now more on an *unconscious* than on a conscious plane. It resembles more the behaviour of animals who passively adapt themselves to their environment. It is far remote from the behaviour of humans who have the potentiality to play an active role in shaping the environment according to their needs and aspirations. And the two elemental forces unconsciously influencing the behaviour of people in the post-independence period seem to be *fear* and *envy*—fear of *insecurity* and envy of the *nouveaux riche*. Human energy released merely as a negative response to fear and envy cannot be truly creative. In order to evoke a positive response from the people and to tap the vast reserves of their creative energy, it is necessary to initiate a process of remoulding of their social outlook. For centuries the masses have been under the influence of myths and ideologies which have sought to reconcile them to their lot and to inculcate in them a paralysing sense of their powerlessness before their fate or their masters. What is needed now is not only a demolition of these myths and ideologies but a positive re-education of the people in terms of a new world-view which remoulds their view of the world and of their own place in it and which also affirms the possibility of having a better world.

For centuries the masses have believed (or have been conditioned to believe) that the injustices of the world can be corrected only by *avatars* and man has only to wait for such *avatars* to be born for the deliverance of humanity from tyranny and oppression. They have now to be helped to have a this-wordly and activist interpretation of the *avatars* as another name for their collective self-realisation of their own latent powers. In other words, a positive response from the people requires a total re-orientation of their world-view. Such cultural re-birth of the people, however, is achieved only in the process of active and close interaction between the dynamic minority (or the elite) and the people as a whole. Earlier we raised the question of the superstructure because this process of interaction is seriously thwarted by powerful factors operating at the level of the superstructure. Any genuine cultural rejuvenation of the people cannot even be contemplated without an effective neutralisation of these factors.

Before taking up the issue of the obstacles it is necessary first to clarify our approach to this question of cultural renewal itself. Indeed the question of cultural renewal can be raised from divergent standpoints. It can be raised by people having different or even opposite standpoints. We reject all those approaches which raise the question of cultural renewal in isolation from the question of *political* awakening of the masses. In our view such approaches are defective as they detach the question of culture from the question of *power*. In fact, what direction does one consciously impart to the process of cultural renewal depends on having or not having a political aim. The forces of cultural renewal can be channelised in the direction of a change in the political balance in favour of the masses. Or, alternatively they can also be channelised in the direction of reinforcing the present political balance which favours the vested interests. In other words, cultural renewal can be linked with political passivity or with political activity of the masses. In our framework of analysis, cultural revitalisation is linked clearly and explicitly with the aim of breaking the passivity of the masses and to activise them as a political force.

This explanation is necessary because of considerable misunderstanding or lack of understanding on this issue even among parties and groups espousing the cause of the masses. These parties and groups are inclined to think that to raise the very question of culture is to raise a non-political question, or a question which diverts the attention of the masses from primary to secondary issues. They would even suggest that the key to cultural awakening lies in political awakening.

Such a summary disposal of the question of cultural renewal only means that these parties and groups fail to appreciate how cultural backwardness of the masses has retarded their political awakening; and how it continues to thwart their political initiative. *To believe in the possibility of the active role of the masses without their cultural awakening is to fail to draw proper lessons from past history*. On the basis of past experience it can be said that not to tackle the problem of cultural backwardness of the masses is to perpetuate also their political backwardness. It is to keep them away from developing the capacity for political initiative as well as for political leadership. No doubt, the process of social and political awakening of the masses is always initiated by the enlightened elements from the upper or the intermediate classes. But can it become self-sustaining without creating from within the masses an intelligentsia actively interacting with them and capable of leading them from darkness to enlightenment? We have in mind an elite which rises in the very process of culturally lifting up the masses from whom it has sprung up rather than rising at their expense or in their name.

Perhaps no other factor delayed the process of the political activisation of the masses so much as the factor of their cultural backwardness. For, the latter has meant a tremendous lag in the formation of an intelligentsia from within the peasantry and the working class. An insufficient attention to the problems of development of such an intelligentsia remains perhaps the basic weakness of the Indian political and social system. It has been neglected by almost all types of political forces committed to modern development in India.

In order to understand the gravity of this problem and its wide ramifications, it is necessary to reckon with certain hard realities of the Indian society. These relate to the problems created by two unique factors operating in India, the existence of most hierarchical social systems, on the one hand, and the history of direct colonialism, on the other. Both conspired to create deep inner schisms in the Indian society the like of which existed in perhaps no other country of the world. Economic and political dominance of the havenots by the haves has been known in most countries. But in no other country was the principle of inequality between man and man implemented with such subtlety and thoroughness as in India. Here the most thorough-going religious indoctrination of the people in the sanctity of inequality was combined with the most pervasive institutional framework of caste ensuring the enforcement of inequality at every moment and in all spheres. In no other country perhaps did man show so much intellectual ingenuity in devising elaborate ideological and institutional devices for discrimination between man and man; and in rationalising and buttressing–through myths, ideologies, values, norms, rules, regulations, rituals, customs and social practices the complete subjection of man by man.

In India, perhaps, was practised as in no other country the worst form of degradation and tyranny ever invented by man and imposed on his fellow beings. This took the form of legitimising through religion and social system the keeping of the masses, away from light and into darkness; and denying them the very opportunity for cultural enlightenment. It amounted virtually to denying them the opportunity to grow as human beings for human beings realise fully their potentialities as human beings only through cultural development.

The Indian masses for thousands of years were conditioned to accept this denial as the consequence of their past sins and as the affirmation of the will of God. *The worst aspect of slavery is the mental bondage of the slave; the slave begins to hug his own fetters. This is exactly what was achieved in India by religion and caste together.* Here the masses seemed to lack even the consciousness of their loss and deprivation. Religion in India acted beyond doubt as the opium of the people.

To believe that such lack of consciousness or such false consciousness of the masses would automatically disappear with the passage of time is to indulge in self-delusion. It is to evade the agonising task of reconditioning and remoulding the minds of millions of human beings. *This liberation from mental bondages, this craving for rebirth as human beings is what is implied in the concept of cultural renewal.*

That this is a qualitatively different approach to the economic, social and political problem of the masses in India needs to be further explained and emphasised. For, the Indian elite has been accustomed to certain habits of thought which have hampered an adequate understanding of the complex nature of the problem of mass emancipation. Here a crude materialism, a vulgar economic interpretation of history have blurred the perception of the importance of the cultural factor. No doubt the economic *factor* is basic in the backwardness of the masses and it is idle to imagine that this backwardness can be eliminated without operating effectively on the economic plane. But this crude materialism overlooks another crucial aspect of the situation. The economic structure which reduces the masses to the status of havenots is maintained and buttressed, among other things, by an ideological or cultural superstructure. The class division between haves and havenots is perpetuated by denying the havenots the cultural means of acquiring a true consciousness of their loss. It is perpetuated by creating a false consciousness among them of their social existence. It is for this reason that any genuine movement for a revolutionary change in the economic structure of society begins as a cultural movement, i.e. it begins at the level of the superstructure.

Class structure thus assumes the sharpest form on the plane of culture, of ideas. It is the most painful when it is fought out inside the minds of men, on the plane of ways of life, habits of thought, values, norms, rules, regulations, rituals and relations between human beings. A cultural revolution is, in this sense, the sharpest expression of struggle between the haves and the havenots. The havenots cannot hope to break away from economic and political dominance of the haves without first breaking away from their cultural hegemony.

Once again we must draw attention to the distinction between animals and human beings. In the subjugation of animals, exercise of crude force is the most important factor. In the subjugation of human beings, exercise of crude force or economic compulsion is not enough. It has to be combined with influence over the minds of men. Ruling classes in class societies, therefore, have had at their service intellectual elites or ideologists and myth-makers creating elaborate rationalisation of exploitation and oppression of havenots by the haves. The first condition of emancipation of the havenots in this background is the rise of critical intellectuals who question the ruling ideologies and myths and try to reveal the true nature of social reality to the masses. The first challenge to the rule of the haves, therefore, emerges on an intellectual or cultural plane. The tempo of changes in the economic struggle and the balance of political forces would always be slowed down if there is *no prior* or *simultaneous* preparation on the cultural plane.

In India such a critical-cultural movement has been thwarted or delayed as a result of the peculiarities of Indian history and social structure. Even when the rudiments of such a critique have appeared, the transmission of these critical-cultural impulses from the questioning minority to the vast masses has been thwarted by powerful obstacles. *India is a typical case of a thwarted or delayed cultural renewal. And the causes of this require a serious scientific investigation.*

3

Class and Social Transformation in India: Possibilities and Constraints of Intermediate Classes

> The task of influencing the vacillators is not identical with the task of overthrowing the exploiters and defeating the active enemy.
>
> — Lenin, 1918.

> Force can be employed against enemies, but not against a part of one's own side which one wishes rapidly to assimilate and whose goodwill and enthusiasm one needs.
>
> — Antonio Gramsci, *Selections From Prison Notebooks*, 1932.

I

The study of the paths of social transformation in the Asian countries is closely related to an analysis of their class structures. The study of classes offers a promising field to Asian social scientists for the creative application of the Marxian theory of classes. It is only in the recent period that professional social scientists in India are beginning to show some interest in examining the relevance of class theory as a tool of macro-sociological and political-economic analysis.[1]

It should be stressed at the very outset that without a serious effort both on theoretical and empirical planes, it is well-nigh impossible to exploit the full potentialities of class analysis for comprehending and even predicting social and political changes in countries like India. For, here a sharp break is required from the habits of conducting class analysis without adequate reference to the concrete realities of the Indian situation which has been so common not only among political activists and Marxist scholars but also among non-Marxist radicals among social scientists. Some of these activists and scholars have also been accustomed to fit in a mechanical manner the facts of the Indian reality into readymade analytical categories and models evolved by Marxist thinkers for Western Europe, USSR or China. This mechanical parallelism has generally hampered perception of the specific features of the social, economic and political evolution in India. Moreover, the crudities, if not falsities, of predictions which arose out of an uncritical and uncreative use of class theory are in the Indian case too numerous and glaring to be dismissed as occasional errors of cognition. It must be admitted that the mechanical use of the class theory has brought this theory itself into disrepute. It has also helped the opponents of class theory to create all-round scepticism about its relevance to Indian conditions. Here is a typical case of wrong or faulty use of a fine instrument leading to the rejection of the instrument itself; a case of the baby being thrown out with the bath water. Social science is thus deprived of a powerful tool for a scientific study of society and its evolution from a lower to a higher stage. In this background the assumptions of the autonomy of the political or social system and the non-class interpretations of social and political phenomena[2] have also gained wide currency among social scientists. This development can be attributed partly, if not wholly, to the failure of class theorists to take adequate cognisance of the complexities of the class situation in countries like India and to introduce appropriate modification or development of the conception of classes in the light of these complexities.[3]

In this paper an attempt has first been made to raise some general issues concerning the study of classes which are relevant for a realistic understanding of the Indian social situation after India's independence from colonial rule. These general issues have been substantiated with illustration from some of the important studies of class and society in India since independence. In the second place, having identified the *intermediate classes* as a distinctive feature of the Indian class structure this paper also evaluates the possibilities and constraints of the *intermediate classes*.

In the recent period a number of social scientists and political leaders have attempted an analysis of the class structure in India for an understanding of the social situation and for predicting the trends of economic, social and political change. These studies have played an outstanding role in bringing to light the class cleavages and conflicts which exist in Indian society and which lie at the root of many social and political movements in recent Indian history. At the same time, even a preliminary survey of these studies is sufficient to convince any disinterested reader that many of these analytical exercises, even though presenting valuable insights, have in certain fundamental respects proved to be inadequate, if not sometimes also misleading; and that their predictions have been belied by the actual course of development. It is not our intention to present here a full critique of these studies; our limited aim is to identify some basic aspects of the approach underlying these studies which vitiate a proper perception of the class structure and of the recent social and political trends in India.

In our view some of the important aspects of the approach underlying studies of classes and socio-economic trends in India can be identified as follows:

1. Most studies present a dichotomic view of classes and class contradictions which tends to underplay the multiplicity of classes and class contradictions.
2. Even when multiplicity is conceded, the emphasis is on the inevitability of economic polarisation leading to political polarisation. The basic premise here is the decline in the significance of the intermediate strata on the economic plane which is assumed to lead to an erosion of middle-of-the-road trends on the political plane. A simplistic view of classes is, therefore, related to a simplistic view of politics. This conception of the declining significance

of the intermediate classes is, therefore, not in consonance with the facts of the Indian situation as revealed by many studies and surveys. In fact, intermediate classes not only continue to exist as an important social category in the Indian social structure; the increasing proliferation and prominence of these classes has been one of the basic tendencies of the Indian situation.

3. The analysis of the impact of technological, social and political factors also starts from a rigid assumption of class polarisation being strengthened by these exogenous factors. This assumption is open to question both on logical and empirical grounds. In industry, agriculture and trade, technological progress has shown unprecedented possibilities of stabilising and promoting, rather than disintegrating and eliminating, the intermediate classes of small and middle entrepreneurs. Similarly, the political imperatives of a multiparty and multi-class parliamentary democratic system, based on adult franchise, also ensures state support and protection to the intermediate classes. The very size of the country and the existence of state governments upholding regional identity also give impetus to proliferation of these intermediate classes in each region rather than to their expropriation and thus to polarisation on all-India plane. We need a new view of social dynamics in the light of a reappraisal of the impact of techno-economic and political processes on class formation in India.
4. Further, the class theorists have also not fully grasped the much more significant role which science and technology— and, therefore, education and culture in the widest sense— are destined to play in the development of underdeveloped countries in the contemporary period. This factor tends to throw up the intelligentsia (the teachers in schools, colleges and university and the research workers in institutes of natural and scientific research) into an enormously important and growing social stratum in the developing countries. Equally important are the rapidly-

growing numbers of the skilled personnel, professionals and technocrats at various levels. Similarly, as a consequence of the pivotal role assigned to the state in economic development and nation-building the bureaucracy also emerges as a powerful and growing social category in most developing countries. Within the bureaucracy itself there is a restratification resulting in the possibility of a greater weightage assigned to those managing the economy in place of the old-style bureaucracy discharging merely the function of maintaining law and order and the extraction of taxes and revenues from the governed classes.

The pressure for operating welfare schemes, e.g. housing, health, nutrition and family-planning and education even at a low stage of economic development, adds vastly to the numbers of technicians and economic and social administrators. Further, the rise of the political party, the parliament, the legislature and the panchayati raj has thrown up the *politician as a new social class* which constitutes one of the most significant contributors to the intermediate classes in the recent period. An important feature of this class of the politician should be noted. In sharp contrast to the economic entrepreneurs, the bureaucracy, the skilled technocracy, the intelligentsia and the armed forces, the recruitment to the political sector is relatively more open. It does not make high demands in terms of educational qualifications and economic power. As a result, in India many who later emerged as influential members of the power-elite—as economic entrepreneurs or as distinguished members of the bureaucracy—did not begin as members of these privileged social strata; they began first as members of a political party. Their rise to economic or administrative or political power was facilitated via their joining a political party or, more specifically, the ruling party. The political process has in this way brought about substantial expansion of the intermediate classes in India. Similarly, the emergence of the trade unions as a powerful social group has also pushed into prominence the trade-union leader as a distinguished entrant into the intermediate classes in India.

To sum up, the vastly changed social situation in India after independence has thrown into prominence *a new middle class* which is potentially capable of a more productive role than the old colonial middle class having a predominantly parasitic orientation. Attempts at class analysis of the Indian social situation have not given due recognition to the emergence of these new class formations which denote the possibility of a new role for the middle classes and strata. What precise role these classes and strata are playing in India is a matter for empirical inquiry. Whether their productive or parasitical potentialities are being actually realised is also a matter of empirical inquiry. But it is obvious that their very existence and growth require a new model of class analysis for analysing the processes of social and economic change.

5. It should also be noted that the model of social change generally in vogue among Marxists has been the two class model of an ascendant capitalism as developed in Volume I of Marx's *Capital*. Seldom has an attempt been made to draw upon Volume III of *Capital* which provides valuable clues for evolving a multi-class model suitable for a society in transition from a pre-industrial to an industrial society. Even here there can be no mechanical imitation of a multiclass model as developed by Marx, for instance, for the French society in his The Eighteenth Brumaire of Louis Bonaparte.

In the case of countries like India which are trying to effect this transition in the second half of the twentieth century the social character and direction of this transition is not predetermined but is to be influenced through conscious choice and social intervention. The task of a social scientist is not, therefore, merely interpretative; interpretation is interlinked here with a normative standpoint. In the studies of past patterns of transition, the social scientist is by and large an analyst outside the social process which he is analysing. In the case of present-day societies the transition has multiple possibilities. It has yet to crystallise into a well-defined pattern. The analyst here is both an outsider as well as an insider to this process. "All theory is grey and only the tree of life is green"—this observation of Goethe is fully applicable to the situation of these countries. Here life has time and again thrown up new features unanticipated by theory which is after all a generalisation of past experience. It is not surprising if the prediction derived from such a theory is not realised. *For, the question in these countries is not just that of exploring conformity of the evolving process to this or that past pattern. It is a question of combining a knowledge of past history with an imaginative perception of future possibilities so as to capture at least some of the new features of the emerging pattern.*

This is not to say that the present is totally independent of the past or that the understanding of the past has no contribution to make to the perception of the emerging pattern. Undoubtedly the emerging situation in countries like India represents a blending of the old and the new. There are, therefore, elements both of a continuity and discontinuity. Insofar as the past itself exercises a pull and insofar as the new forces may not enjoy adequate autonomy or force to compel a break from the past, the emerging pattern may have more of the old than of the new. It may at best denote a certain variation of the old pattern only. But insofar as a developing country like India is favourably placed both exogenously as well as endogenously to generate enough momentum for growth on new lines, the new elements may outweigh the old and thus hold possibilities of throwing up a new balance of class forces resulting in a new pattern of development.

One of the basic weaknesses of recent class analysis of India has been that the analysts have fallen a prey to the temptation of *looking for continuity of the past or for conformity to past patterns of development instead of exploring discontinuity or departures from the classical patterns.* Since these analysts have also been leaders of the social and political movements, their failure is not just on the academic plane. It cannot be ruled out that such surrender to crude determinism is bound to have prevented these activists from grasping new possibilities for a break from the classical patterns and for giving a conscious turn to Indian history. Intellectual conformism or dogmatism thus results in the very opposite of what Marxism stands for. Such overdeterministic Marxism repudiates the very spirit of Marx. It turns into a modern version of fatalism. It leads to reducing man into the object rather than the subject of historical movement.

If the Indian situation continues to offer possibilities of crystallisation of a new pattern, it is because the Marxist activists are not the sole custodians of intervention in historical change. At the same time, if the Indian situation has not yet decisively turned in favour of the possibilities of a fully non-classical pattern and has time and again created the fear of a retrogression, it is because of lack of full mobilisation of the social forces for such a new pattern. And the fatalistic conception of Marxism[4] must bear part if not the whole blame for the failure to capitalise on a series of opportunities in India.

It should be noted that the aim of this article is not to attempt an empirical examination of Indian society since independence in the light of the above observations and hypotheses. It is only to show how many attempts by outstanding Marxist scholars and other radical social scientists have proved inadequate because of a rigid adherence to a mechanistic class theory. In the next section of this paper we draw upon some of the class interpretations of the Indian development since independence for illustrating some of the points made above.

II

In support of our statement that the dichotomic view of classes is common to most studies, reference can be made to two studies—one by E.M.S. Namboodiripad and the other by Gunnar Myrdal.

While making a broad generalisation about the changing pattern of class relations in India since independence, Namboodiripad observes:

> Here, therefore, is a situation in which two combinations of classes are slowly shaping themselves and facing each other—those who share, or at least have the illusion of sharing, economic and political power on one hand and those that are deprived of, and are conscious of being deprived of, that power. Among the former are the bourgeois proper, the ex-feudal or other landlords who are today closer than ever before to the bourgeoisie and the new elements in the rural and urban society, who help to ascend the ladder of the newly-rising bourgeois society. Among the latter are the overwhelming majority of the people, the workers, the peasants, the artisans and the other small property owners, the toiling middle classes and also others who feel the heavy burden of landlord-capitalist exploitation.[5]

Namboodiripad is not unaware of the 'contradictions and conflicts' within each of these two major class combinations. But he considers the conflict between the two class combinations as the primary and the other conflicts as secondary from a long-term point of view. To quote: "Neither of these two camps, however, is completely unified within itself. There are conflicts, contradictions and struggles within each, though these are subordinated, in the long run, to the common interests of their respective class combinations."[6]

Namboodiripad further asserts that: "... the landlords, the bourgeoisie and their allies are bound to compose their differences and fight the common people unitedly whenever the latter become sufficiently organised and powerful to challenge the present regime".[7]

The above diagnosis of the class situation leads Namboodiripad to suggest the inevitability of a shift either to the left or to the right in Indian politics.[8]

A dichotomic view of classes also characterises Myrdal's analysis of the Indian situation. To quote:

> As we constantly stress, all social mechanisms in India operate mainly in accordance with the power structure. India is ruled by compromises and accommodations within and between the upper-upper class and various groups that constitute the bulk of the upper class. The fact that the members of the upper class call themselves, and believe themselves to be 'middle class' is not without significance... . The government has tried by various means, including a progressive income tax, to limit the power and wealth of the upper-upper class—the maharajas, the landlords, the tycoons in industry and finance. The upper strata of the landowners in the villages, the traders and moneylenders, the ordinary industrialists, and the civil servants below the very top level look on these policies, which incidentally have not been very effective, as attempts to establish greater equality. In public discussion it is commonly argued that greater consideration of the middle class could further the cause of equality. The truth is of course that in the Indian setting, this 'middle class' is definitely upper class. It is the lower class that needs to be aided if there is to be a real advance in equality.[9]

Myrdal believes that so far as the class and power situation in the underdeveloped countries is concerned, "there is little difference between the countries that have succeeded in establishing and retaining a system of parliamentary democracy and those that by 'revolution' have brought to power an authoritarian government of one type or another." In his view, "power almost always belongs to varying sections of the upper class, taken in its wider meaning as including the so-called middle class."[10]

Myrdal also suggests that non-economic factors like population growth tend to further widen the gap between the upper class and the poverty-stricken masses.[11] Further economic factors like the new technology and the green revolution also tend to reinforce this hiatus between the upper and the lower classes.[12] In fact, growing economic polarisation emerges in Myrdal's analysis as the logical consequence of economic development within the framework of a sharply dichotomic class and power structure.

Unlike Namboodiripad, however, Myrdal does not suggest any inevitable link between growing economic inequality and political polarisation. Myrdal observes: "What is lacking in India is organised pressure from below on the part of the masses of people."[13]

The lower classes, are, therefore, mobilised generally in the interests of different sections of the upper class but seldom in defence of their own interests. In such a situation "there is quite clearly a possibility or even perhaps a probability that in India or indeed in the larger part of South Asia there will be neither much evolution nor revolution".[14]

Apart from the studies by Myrdal and Namboodiripad, there are studies by Charles Bettelheim,[15] Paul A. Baran,[16] Barrington Moore Jr.[17], Kathleen Gough[18] and a host of other scholars which reflect a somewhat similar orientation and approach. Even when they draw attention to certain distinctive features of the Indian class situation, they do not attach much weight to them in their assessment of the overall economic and political trends in India. Their work cannot be questioned on the ground of fidelity to facts. What is questionable, therefore, is the significance attached to one set of facts as against another set of facts. What is less satisfying is the theory of classes underlying their interpretations.

Namboodiripad, for instance, draws attention to the rise of new and dynamic sections from the hitherto oppressed and impoverished classes "who are able to get better jobs, make greater profits and aspire for bigger prospects of development which could never have been imagined in the pre-independence years or even in the years before the Second Five Year Plan." He observes that their "interests are in fundamental conflict with those of the landlords and the capitalists who are in control of the state and dominating the economy of the country." These classes and strata are thus "interested in the full elimination of all forms of feudal exploitation (rent, usury, bonded-labour, etc.) which is hampered by the compromise that has been struck between the feudal and the capitalist elements of the ruling class."[19]

Having made these highly perceptive observations regarding the potentialities of these classes in the fight against big landlord-capitalist exploitation, Namboodiripad, however, draws the opposite political conclusion in his overall assessment. He regards these new sections as allies of the upper classes rather than of the working masses. Namboodiripad thereby indirectly suggests that the principal contradiction in Indian society is between the upper, the new intermediate classes, on the one hand and the small propertied and toiling masses, on the other. *He does not conform to the view that the principal contradiction in Indian society is between all genuinely productive classes including the new middle class, on the one hand and the wholly parasitic and unproductive classes thriving on usury, landed property and mercantile-capitalist exploitation, on the other.* In other words, overlooking totally the context of an underdeveloped, ex-colonial society, Namboodiripad denies any progressive potentialities to those very intermediate classes and social strata whom he, with his sound empirical sense, identified as a new feature of India's class structure since independence.

Charles Bettelheim, in his well-known work *India Independent*, shows a penetrating insight into some of the important features of the Indian economic and social situation. One of his important observations pertains to the growth of small and medium enterprises in agriculture, commerce and industry. He notes that "the development of credit cooperatives, the creation of the State Bank and of the various public financial institutions, etc. have simultaneously helped to develop agricultural capitalism and small industrial capitalism."[20] Analysing the significance of it he observes: "In this sense, recent development has certainly enlarged the social base of Indian capitalism. This is one of the social and economic reasons why the Congress Party has remained united, despite a number of minor crises, and why a second big party upholding the big bourgeoisie's interests has not yet gained much strength."[21]

In spite of the great caution exercised by Bettelheim in drawing conclusions and in making generalisations, his analysis, however, not only underplays the significance of the new middle classes in Indian society; he also denies the sharpness of its conflict with the upper classes. He tends time and again, in spite of habitual caution, to refer to "class polarisation,"[22] to the possibility of a violent opposition among the people and the weakening of the parliamentary system which could lead to dictatorship."[23] He also emphasises the fact of "solidarity among the privileged class" which, in his opinion, "is too great for any of these classes to eliminate the precapitalist struc-tures."[24] Having said this, however, Bettelheim adds that "the Indian bourgeoisie has made greater attempts to eliminate these structures than has the bourgeoisie of any other country."[25]

In our view the central weakness of all these analyses of the Indian class situation is that they do not seem to recognise *the emergence of the new middle class—as distinct from the traditional upper class—as an important social category and as the most decisive factor in the economic, social and political transformation of India since independence.* It is the new middle class which provides the distinguishing feature of the Indian class structure. India, therefore, emerges as a somewhat unique type in the Asian context—a type which has perhaps no parallel in other parts of Asia.

Scholars have generally tended to place India within a general type—a procedure which eliminates rather than highlights the uniqueness of the Indian situation. In fact, the neocolonialist type of class and political situation, characterised by the leading role of a conservative and reactionary upper class, was typified not by India but by Pakistan.[26] In other words, the model of cumulative class conflict and sharp polarisation which has been wrongly applied to India by many scholars is far more relevant for the old Pakistan.

And applied to Pakistan even the predictions by social scientists about polarisation leading to an explosive political situation assume a truly prophetic quality.

So far as India is concerned, the formation of the new middle class and the role of this class, its possibilities and constraints for Indian national development and social transformation, require an objective analysis and assessment. There are two distinct types of errors which are possible in evaluating the political and social possibilities of these intermediate classes and strata. The first error is that committed by social theorists and political representatives of these intermediate classes and strata. They nurse the illusion that these classes and strata are themselves capable of providing the leadership in the transition to a modern society and of accomplishing this transition. Indian historical experience during the last twenty-five years has shown that these classes and strata are undoubtedly capable of initiating this process and taking it forward. But, left to themselves, they do not seem capable of imparting to it the necessary momentum and of completing it.

The second type of error is committed by Marxist theorists who tend to believe that these classes and strata have no independent role to play and are very soon swallowed up or at least severely constrained by the inertia, overwhelming conservatism and power of vested interests of the traditional society. They are not even capable of serving as dependable allies in this historic transition to a modern society.

Both these types of interpretations are inadequate as complete interpretations even though each captures a partial facet of the reality. The error lies in blowing up the partial view into a total view. For a proper evaluation it is necessary to identify the basic potentialities as well as the constraints of the intermediate classes and strata. If the middle-of-the-road ideologists exaggerate the potentialities of the intermediate classes and strata, the left ideologists have tended to denigrate them. Similarly, if the ideologues of centrism have tended to overlook the constraints, the left ideologues have tended to exaggerate them.

The positive potentialities of the intermediate classes and social strata can be assessed only from a historical perspective.

It must not be overlooked that after the total defeat of the 1857 "mutiny" at the hands of the superior forces of the British colonialists the native upper classes gave up the path of resistance to British rule and, in fact, turned into an ally or into the bulwark of the British colonialist system in India. *The possibilities of a Japanese pattern of industrial-capitalist transition led by a renovated upper class were thus completely thwarted by the peculiarities of Indian historical development.* The leadership to the anti-imperialist multiclass national revolution was, therefore, provided by the intermediate classes and social strata. They played the decisive role in unifying the different classes of Indian society and in evolving diverse forms of resistance against imperialism. In this process these classes also became the historical instrument of a vast, unprecedented awakening among the toiling millions of India, specially among the teeming millions living in India's villages. These classes and social strata were able to throw up a leader of the stature of Mahatma Gandhi who was uniquely suited to play this role of unifier of the nation as well as an energiser of the peasantry. In other words, these classes and social strata historically served not only as an instrument of the *national revolution*; they have also served as a bridge between the *national revolution* based on the unity of all the classes and a *social revolution* decisively upholding the interests of the most oppressed classes of workers and peasants.

From Ram Mohun Roy, the father of modern India, to Indira Gandhi, these classes and social strata have been able to throw up a galaxy of outstanding leaders who have played a leading role not only in pulling the Indian people out of the colonialist bondage and consolidating Indian freedom; they have also served objectively as the decisive factor in generating urges and aspirations among the masses for a fundamental social transformation.

In no other country which won its freedom from colonial rule after the Second World War have the intermediate classes and strata been instruments of such historically significant changes and developments as in India. To ignore this role of the intermediate classes and strata in India is to depart very seriously from historical objectivity.

Having emphasised the positive potentialities of these classes and strata it is also necessary to identify their constraints which have prevented these potentialities from turning into actual accomplishments. And in this respect the three weaknesses of these classes indicated below are very crucial.

The first weakness arises from the inadequate economic and cultural dissociation or break of these classes and social strata from the traditional upper classes. Historically these classes and social strata originated in the context of a colonial economy and as a result they had a non-producer and parasitical bias. There is no doubt that in India after independence there emerged a more favourable framework for the break from parasitism and for the emergence of a more genuine middle class. But in most regions like West Bengal, Bihar, East and Central UP, etc. which were historically exposed much more to the corrosive effects of colonial and feudal domination in economic and cultural spheres, the growth of such a genuine non-parasitical middle class has been much slower than in the relatively somewhat more dynamic regions like Punjab, Haryana, West UP, etc. Taking the country as a whole, however, the intermediate classes and social strata have been severely constrained by parasitism from ensuring a full release of productive forces and creative energies.

What is generally termed as lack of political will of these classes and social strata is most often a lack of courage to shake off the deadweight of parasitism and to merge their destiny and share the burdens and fruits of freedom with the common masses. In another paper I have tried to explain the genesis of this parasitic orientation and its relation to the internal class structure, influence from affluent countries and to strong remnants of colonial and feudal culture.[27] What needs to be reiterated, however, is the use of the state and the power structure for parasitic extortion rather than for combating parasitism with a view to ensuring an all-out mobilisation of social forces for the growth of the economy. What is worse is that at strategic points of the power structure there is subversion of programmes having the objective of combating parasitism. Equally serious is the parasitic distortion of the development process itself. *Thus there is often the appearance of growth without the substance of self-sustaining growth*; there is often what Bettleheim calls pseudo-industrialisation rather than genuine industrialisation.

It must be recognised that, historically speaking, the severest indictment of parasitism of Indian society also came from the tallest leader produced by the intermediate classes and social strata themselves. It must also be recognised that parasitism is not so nakedly flaunted in India as in some of the upper-class regimes in the Asian countries. The intermediate classes and social strata in India also carry a growing sense of guilt about it. If their anti-parasitical consciousness has not developed into a powerful social force, it is because the intermediate classes and social strata have not yet broken the umbilical cord connecting them with the upper classes. They have not yet decisively linked themselves to the genuine non-parasitic elements of Indian society, viz. the toiling peasants and labourers. There can be no emergence of anti-parasitism through practice of anti-parasitism into a social movement at an individual or group level only even though it is an important prerequisite for it. What is required for it is the political activation of the non-parasitic classes for a new path of development. The failure to attempt this explains the failure of all types of political forces committed to fundamental social change in India.

The second major weakness of the intermediate classes and social strata has been their compromise with elitism which is another index of their inadequate break from the traditional upper class and from the old type of unproductive middle classes. Elitism reflects an escape from the hard and agonising task of resolving the question of values, of discarding old values and evolving new ones appropriate to the needs of society in a dynamic context. Elitism is an escape from genuine value choice into either a blind worship of one's past culture or the equally slavish imitation of the West. On the one hand, elitism is an escape from the vital currents of past tradition into attachment to its formal aspects. On the other hand, it is an incapacity to grasp the fundamental ideals of the West but imitate only its outward and less important aspects. A break from elitism is, therefore, only partly a negative process of rejecting certain values and the way of life based on these values. More fundamental is the *positive aspect of building up a new value system and a new way of life.* This itself cannot be done in a socio-cultural vacuum but with reference to the concrete realities and the challenges of our own society. With a view to shaking off the attributes of elitism and to initiate the process of transforming themselves into a genuine ruling elite, the intermediate classes and social strata need to link themselves to the toiling masses, to the workers and the peasants. They need to rededicate themselves to the service, uplift and enlightenment of the toiling masses. *A way of life not above the masses or at the expense of the masses but in the service of the masses alone can be the basis of an intellectual and cultural renewal of the intermediate classes and social strata.*

A genuine break from elitism, however, is not possible without accelerating the formation of a new intelligentsia from among the toiling masses. And this calls for a total reorientation of the educational system in the country. The perpetuation of an English-knowing, Westernised intelligentsia which is neither willing nor capable of assimilating and disseminating modern knowledge in the language of the people is the most powerful factor for the continuing urban-rural hiatus and is perhaps the most favourable soil for the perpetuation of elitism. The neglect of primary and secondary education and adult literacy in rural areas, and the massive exodus of the able-bodied and talented persons from the villages to the towns and the general resistance to live and work in the villages, among the elite are factors which perpetuate this urban-rural hiatus. They also thwart the emergence of an earth-bound intelligentsia from among the peasantry which can break through this rural-urban cleavage and pave the basis for a more dynamic and productive interaction between the towns and the villages.

The third major weakness of the intermediate classes and social strata has been *softness* in dealing with hard choices and dilemmas posed by the process of development. This *softness* has many ramifications. In the post-independence period the character-type thrown up by these classes and strata is that of a skilled operator nakedly pursuing power in the narrow sense rather than a social worker achieving power through service. Another significant feature has been the tendency to succumb easily to the pressure from those having a vested interest in the *status quo* rather than resist it firmly and meet it by mobilising counterpressure from those having an interest in change and growth. The premium on manipulative politics and the disregard for mass politics stabilises the soft character-type, there being no mechanism now after independence for weeding out soft elements in the political sphere. In the pre-independence period the increasing compulsions of struggle and sacrifice did not permit the soft character-type to strike deep root in the Indian political life. The parliamentary system and its particular interpretation by the dominant elite in terms of rejection of extra-parliamentary struggle and mobilisation has allowed softness to become a chronic constraint of the elite. Further, the absence of any serious threat to the power of the dominant elite from other contenders for power has allowed softness to become a chronic national malady rather than a sectional aberration. With softness goes also aversion to sharing the burdens of hardships of growth, and to undertake the hard task of building cadres and organising the oppressed classes for defence of their rights and discharge of their duties.

Another significant aspect of softness is the incapacity to be outspoken and exacting with the people when the need arises, to lead rather than to be led by the masses on such occasions. Thus arises the ambivalence so characteristic of the intermediate classes and social strata—the continuing articulation of support to certain principles but the infirmity expressed in implementing these principles. Softness is also manifest, therefore, in resort to demagogy to cover up the vacillations at the level of practice.

In fact, this variety of softness as reflected in regarding the enunciation of an idea itself as an act or a deed does not find such classic expression perhaps in any other country as in India. (This is quite in line with the magical powers that are attributed to 'mantras' or to words in classical Brahmanical rituals.)

The most dangerous aspect of softness is reflected in the incapacity of the political elite to be self-exacting; more importantly, it is reflected in its incapacity to be self-critical in the true sense. Hypocritical self-criticism is the rule now in a parliamentary regime. Self-criticism here "offers opportunity for fine speeches and pointless declarations and for nothing else; self-criticism has been parliamentarised" (Gramsci). In fact, as Gramsci further observes, "such 'implicit' and 'tacit' parliamentarism is far more dangerous than the explicit variety, since it has all its defects without its positive values. *The contribution of parliamentarism to the softening of national character is of enormous importance in a country where parliamentarism has not evolved from within but has been implanted from outside.* It has been grafted on a society which has not yet made a decisive break from feudal and colonial values and ways of life.

Another aspect of softness is reflected in the romanticism with which the intermediate classes and strata approach the hard economic problems or the hard challenges of the economic transition. For, here it is not enough to enunciate correct principles. The battle of principles has to be fought out at the level of details which requires a new blending of political stamina and scientific expertise. Economic planning and policy-making is not the field for the ignoramus but for the competent. Here political will has to be translated ultimately into superior technical competence. In fact, as D.P. Mukerji once observed, it requires a new character-type to make a success of the economic plan. Softness is also reflected sometimes in wishing away the inconvenient aspects of reality rather than boldly recognising them and evolving methods to deal with them.

It is pertinent to refer in this context to another factor which has grown as a reaction to elitism and which reinforces the drive for soft options. This is the phenomenon of *populism* which represents an escape from leading the people and educating them about their role in growth and development. *Populism* is cheap idolatory of the people which has nothing to do with accepting the active role of the people in history. Crude economism is another aspect of populism which is basically rooted in envy of the upper classes and has nothing to do with inculcating a correct moral outlook based on unity of rights and duties. The failure of the leading sections of society to throw up socially-productive and meaningful styles of life and codes of conduct is a major reflection of their basic softness. They try to hide it by further drift into elitism; by a flaunting of outward symbols to be able to exercise authority over the masses. Relapse into elitism or softening of the moral fibre has been invariably associated with decline in moral authority over the masses as every break from softness (or from "elitism" and "parasitism") has always resulted in recapturing of the moral authority.

What are the reasons for softness growing into such a basic and chronic malady of national character? Here it is necessary to make a departure from the tendency to characterise softness as purely a psychological phenomenon, or as the psychological trait of the Hindu mind and Hindu personality. Such pseudo-scientific explanations seem to confuse rather than clarify issues. More importantly, they tend to treat variables as constants; they take not a dynamic but a static view of national character. They tend to underplay, therefore, the possibilities of changing this character by changing the social structure. Insofar as social being determines social consciousness, the latter undergoes a qualitative change if the conditions of social existence are altered through social intervention.

Softness from this point of view is not just a psychological malady. It is a socially-conditioned weakness of character of intermediate classes and social strata arising from the fact that they are not firmly rooted in a productive social existence. If productive labour is the key to a truly moral social existence, insufficient commitment to productive labour does not allow the formation of a wholesome social character. Softness from this standpoint is an expression of a state of alienation in a class society. And it can be overcome only by overcoming this state of alienation. In other words, the more firmly the intermediate classes and social strata return to the principle of a productive social existence, the more thoroughly they succeed in promoting a qualitative transition from *softness* to *strength* of character. The more firmly these classes break from parasitic extortion and turn towards contributing their best to the development of social productivity, the more rapidly would their antagonism as non-producing appropriators with the masses of direct producers also come to an end. With a thorough renovation of the basis of their social existence would follow a full release of their creative energies and a decisive break from a *soft* social personality.

That the softness of the intermediate classes and social strata is closely related to their conditions of social existence can also be derived from the very process of their formation as a class. These classes and social strata are a product both of downward as well as upward social mobility. The ranks of these classes are, on the one hand, swelled by those members of the upper classes—the landed gentry, the mercantile and usurious groups or priestly and warrior castes—whose existence as leisured classes is eroded by the inexorable logic of social and political change. These members are forced to descend to the position of intermediate social strata as professional social strata or business classes. The rank of intermediate classes are also swelled by those members of the lower classes who are fortunate enough to ascend in numerous ways to a higher position, i.e. to the position of intermediate classes. This heterogeneous social composition of the intermediate classes and the circumstances of their genesis as a fluid class explain the mercurial temper, the volatile nature and social unsteadiness which generally characterise these classes. Their transition to extremist moods of exaltation and depression, to negative protest and escapist romanticism and to avoidance of the exacting task of building up a positive social outlook resulting in lack of sustained creativity—all this which finds a crystallised expression in the term *softness* is generally the social-psychology of uprooted groups having a fragmented and fluid class identity.

It should be noted that the nationalist struggle representing more a negative (overthrow of the colonial regime) rather than a positive (construction of a new order) task provided a natural and easy outlet for the pent-up frustrations, ambitions and urges of these intermediate classes and social strata. But this very radicalism, which was a tremendous asset for the nationalist phase, turns into a liability during the phase of national reconstruction and social revolution. For this latter phase what is required is a more positive rather than a merely negative character-type. In this second phase a radical urge has to be blended with a sense of realities; without the latter, the former turns very soon into a source of primitive rebelliousness rather than of revolutionary energy. It only feeds primitive anarchism which has recurrently disrupted and thwarted the revolutionary process in many Asian countries. It has reinforced trends of social retrogression rather than social reorganisation in these countries. But how to ensure that radical sentiment and urge of the intermediate classes and social strata do not turn into a destructive but a positive force has been a major problem in most developing countries.

Space does not allow us to take the problem of transformation of national character for comprehensive analysis. This has been attempted elsewhere. In brief, it is important to take account of the close interaction between the question of transformation of the national character and the question of transformation of the old politico-economic basis. If this interaction is overlooked, one is likely to be lost in the blind alley of such ideologies as "moral rearmament", "anuvrata", radical humanism, etc. In this context lessons should be drawn from the historical experience of countries like Germany and Japan. The general lesson can be summed up in these words: Where modern development has been attempted without a thorough reorganisation of the old politico-economic basis, the socio-cultural remnants of the past hang like a deadweight on the present in the form of such aberrations as "parasitism", "elitism" "softness", etc. An elimination of these aberrations is, therefore, linked with the elimination of the old politico-economic basis. Where there is a gradual adaptation rather than a revolutionary break from the old politico-economic basis, the character traits analysed above arise on the basis of inability of the intermediate classes to break away from the ideology, politics and culture of the upper classes. New character-traits can emerge only in the process of total realignment of the intermediate classes and social strata with worker and peasant masses.

The starting point of this process of realignment by the intermediate classes is the upholding of new normative principles by them. The most important of these are the principles of *assuming responsibility for one's own fate and of productive endeavour as the basis of a moral social existence*. Both the principles of responsibility and of social productivity require a total break from the upper classes (i.e. end of the old politico-economic basis) and a total identification with the toiling worker-peasant masses (i.e. creation of a new politico-economic basis). Affirming the principle of responsibility means attacking the fatalistic outlook at its very roots. It means upholding new culture and politics, i.e. revolutionising the peasant who is the age-old vehicle of the outlook of fatalism. Affirming the principle of productivity means attacking both crude economism as well as primitive anarchism, the two ideological forces undermining the principle of social productivity.

One must recognise that one chapter of the positive role of the intermediate classes and social strata was over with the close of the Nehru era. The next chapter was heralded by the split in the Indian National Congress under the leadership of Indira Gandhi. Whether this political development reflected the stirrings of a critical self-consciousness among the intermediate classes and social strata or a false step is able an open question.

It should be noted, however, that the achievement of a political rectification and renewal on the basis of this critical self-consciousness presupposes a more imaginative and mature response from the representations of the worker-peasant masses. In the absence of such a response temporary setback and retreats of the process of political renewal cannot be ruled out.

Notes and References

1. In the past Marxist political activists applied the class theory to the study of Indian society and to the understanding of the problems of Indian revolution. For such class analyses of the Indian society, in the pre-independence period the most noteworthy are the political theses of the Communist Party of India. The other important references include K.S. Shelvankar's *Problems of India* (1940) and Rajni Palme Dutt's *India Today* (1942). The use of the class theory by professional social scientists has started mostly after independence. The most outstanding and pioneer contribution from this point of view is A.R. Desai's *Social Background of Indian Nationalism* (1959).
   Some of the more recent class analyses of the Indian society are:
   (i) K.N. Raj, "Development Problems of India and Methodology of Karl Marx", Foundation Day Address at the A.N. Sinha Institute of Social Studies, Patna, October 8, 1971 and published in *Mainstream*, Vol. X, No. 8,1971.
   (ii) K.N. Raj, "The Economics and Politics of the Intermediate Regimes", *The Indian Left-Review*, November, 1973.
   (iii) Kathleen Gough, "Peasant Resistance and Revolt in South India, *Pacific Affairs*, Vol. XLI, No. 4, Winter 1963-69.
   (iv) P.C. Joshi, "Agrarian Social Structure and Social Change", *Sankhya, Series* B, Vol. 31, Parts 3 and 4, Indian Statistical Institute, Calcutta, 1969.
   (v) P.C. Joshi, "Land Reform and Agrarian Change in India and Pakistan", in Ratna Datta and P.C. Joshi (ed.), *Studies in Asian Social Development*, New Delhi, 1971.
   (vi) Asok Sen, "Marxism and the Petty-Bourgeois Default", in P.C. Joshi (ed.), *Homage to Karl Marx*, Delhi, 1969.
   (vii) Asok Sen, "Marx, Weber and India Today", *The Economic and Political Weekly*, Vol. VII, Nos. 5, 6 and 7, February 1972.
   (viii) Boudhayan Chattopadhyay, "India's Economic Crisis", in P.C. Joshi (ed.), *Homage to Karl Marx*, Delhi, 1969.
2. Two recent studies on modern India illustrate this trend of non-class interpretation of social and political phenomena. Thus Rajni Kothari in his book, *Politics in India* observes:

"For it is clear neither the traditional sociological nor the traditional economic variables provide adequate categories by which political behaviour can be explained, much less induced. We are investigating a society where change is neither wholly induced by nor is it a reflection of a given balance of forces. Politics in a society like India is at once restricted in its effective social coverage and *autonomous in whatever it covers....* The forms of politics themselves assume a dynamic quality. All this calls for a different framework of analysis that is provided by traditional developmental theory" (p. 12, emphasis added).

While Kothari's critique of crude economic determinism is justified, he has extended this critique to the point of devaluing the significance of the economic factor. Even though the book has a chapter on "Political Economy of Development", the interaction of the political and the economic has not been explored with any seriousness.

Another major work by Louis Dumont, called *Homo Heirarchious, the Caste System and Its Implications* is also characterised by the tendency to devalue the *political-economic basis of the caste system* and to assign a primary or independent role to the *ideological aspect of caste*. Dumont states in clear terms:

"There is scarcely need to repeat that while the aspects called 'politico-economic' are thus considered secondary in relation to the ideology of caste, this is not the result of any prejudice but only of the necessity of giving a faithful picture of the system as it appears to us. It is not impossible, although it is hardly conceivable at present, that in the future politico-economic aspects will be shown to be in reality the fundamental ones and the ideology secondary. Only we are not there yet. For the moment it is a question of a comprehensive description, one which is both intelligent and all-embracing" (p. 39).

At another place in the book Dumont further remarks:

"One can say that just as religion in a way encompasses politics, so politics encompasses economics within itself. The difference is that the politico-economic domain is separated, named, in a subordinate position as against religion, while economics remains undifferentiated from politics" (p. 165).

In support of his view that politico-economic factors are subordinate to caste, Dumont suggests that the Marxian prediction regarding the role of modern industry as a dissolvent of caste was not confirmed by actual developments. To quote: "Given our way of thinking, we must face the fact that the anticipated links between techno-economic change and social change did not operate and that caste society managed to digest what was thought must make it burst asunder. This is the main fact that even the very common overestimation of change has not managed to conceal" (pp. 218-19).

Dumont would have been right if he suggested that Marx's prediction about the introduction of modern transport and communications necessarily leading to the development of modern industry in India was not borne by later development. Colonialism thwarted this possibility of industrial progress. The second prediction regarding the weakening of caste went wrong since the first prediction regarding industrial progress also went wrong. The persistence of caste under British rule therefore does not show that political-economic change was absorbed by caste without itself getting modified in this process. In other words, caste persisted under British rule not because of the force of caste ideology or the power of caste to withstand the onslaught of economic forces. It persisted because of the *peculiar economic conditions obtaining under a colonial economy*—the overpressure in agriculture, the overgrowth of a tertiary sector and the growth of urbanisation without industrialisation, etc.—which sustained and reinforced it. Caste society in a colonial politico-economic framework was of a fundamentally different character than what this caste society was within a traditional economic framework.

Dumont misses the new features of caste because of his "idealist" bias. While those following a non-idealist approach or historical materialist approach would attempt to analyse caste not only in terms of its ideological principles but also in relation to the political-economic basis of caste society Dumont would consider the principles as the determinants of caste even in the politico-economic sphere. His approach amounts to saying: A phenomenon like caste cannot be understood except in terms of the ideology of caste, or in terms of people's own representation of it or consciousness of it. In other words, viewed from the static standpoint of ideology rather than the dynamic standpoint of material life, caste society would give a false impression of continuity and changelessness rather than of fluidity and plasticity.

3. In this respect the following extract from Ossowski is very relevant and illuminating:

"The dichotomic view (of class) is the most convenient for the tasks which the Marxian doctrine was to carry out because of the sharpness of the asymmetrical divisions. On the other hand, large number of social classes is an assumption which is needed for the class interpretation of the complicated processes of history and the whole variety of cultural phenomena. This interpretation which ascribes a many-sided significance to class divisions... cannot be confined within a dichotomic structure. If all political or religious struggles are to be interpreted as class struggle... then we must make use of a greater number of classes than the two basic ones in the *Communist Manifesto*" (Class Structure and Social Consciousness, 1963, pp. 87-88).

4. A brief comment on the fatalistic orientation of Marxism is necessary here. The experience of Marxism in many countries shows that it passes through a phase dominated by "fatalism" and by "mechanism". As Gramsci observes: "When you do not have the initiative in the struggle and the struggle itself comes eventually to be identified with a series of defeats, mechanical determinism becomes a tremendous force of moral resistance, of cohesion and of patient and obstinate resistance. 'I have been defeated for the moment but the tide of history is working for me in the long run.' Real will takes on the garment of an act of faith in a certain rationality of history and in a primitive and empirical form of impassioned finalism which appears in the role of a substitute for the predestination or the providence of confessional religions.. .."

   But Gramsci also emphasises that whatever "usefulness" this fatalistic orientation might have had "for a certain period of history" one might "prepare for its funeral orations". Further: "Its role could really be compared with that of the theory of predestination and grace for the beginnings of the modern world, a theory which finds its culmination in the classical German philosophy and in its conception of freedom as the consciousness of necessity" (Antonio Gramsci, *Selections From Prison Notebooks*, pp. 336-37).

   Whatever role the fatalistic element in Marxism might have played in the past in India in producing a certain sense of confidence in one's cause and a sense of cohesion to the solid forces fighting against formidable odds, it outlived its utility long ago. It is now a cause of what Gramsci calls "weakness of will", or weakness of critical self-consciousness. It causes 'passivity' and 'idiotic self-sufficiency'.
5. E.M.S. Namboodiripad, *Economics and Politics of the Socialist Pattern*, Delhi, 1966, p. 281.
6. Ibid., p. 281.
7. Ibid., p. 283.
8. Ibid., pp. 409-12.
9. Gunnar Myrdal, *Asian Drama, An Enquiry into the Poverty of Nations*, 1968, Vol. II, p. 766.
10. Gunnar Myrdal, *The Challenge of World Poverty*, 1970, p. 398.
11. "The growth of labour force in agriculture has an inherent tendency to increase fragmentation of land holding. More generally, it will tend to force people down the economic and social ladder, making owners tenants and tenants landless workers while the size of the small farms

will decline. Population increase is thus in itself one of the forces that work for increasing social and economic inequality in agriculture" (*The Challenge of World Poverty*, p. 381).

12. "In a country like India, it is a disquieting fact that there are no indications of either policy or research being directed towards the combined objective of labour-intensive and at the same time high-productivity agriculture.

    "The introduction of labour-saving technology will then add its effects to all other developments that tend to increase social and economic inequality in underdeveloped countries and to press down the lower strata in agriculture. The main one is that rapid increase of labour force that is imprisoned in agriculture to the extent that it is now fleeing to the slums in the cities" (*The Challenge of World Poverty*, p. 385).
13. Gunnar Myrdal, Ibid., p. 405.
14. Ibid., p. 412.
15. Charles Bettelheim, *India Independent*, 1963.
16. Paul A. Baran, *The Political Economy of Growth*, India, 1958.
17. Barrington Moore, Jr, *Social Origins of Dictatorship and Democracy*, London, 1967.
18. Kathleen Gough, "Peasant Resistance and Revolt in South India," *Pacific Affairs*, Vol. XII, No. 4, Winter 1968-69, pp. 526-45.
19. E.M.S. Namboodiripad, op cit., pp. 277-78.
20. Charles Bettelheim, op cit., p. 269.
21. Ibid., p. 268.
22. Ibid., p. 360.
23. Ibid., p. 363.
24. Ibid., p. 369.
25. Ibid., p. 369.
26. For a comparative study of power-elite, class structure and patterns of land reforms and agrarian change, see P.C. Joshi, "Land Reform and Agrarian Change in India and Pakistan Since 1947", *Journal of Peasant Studies*, Vol. I, Nos. 2 and 3, January and April 1974.
27. See, P.C. Joshi, "The Cultural Dimension of Economic Development", in Satish Saberwal (ed.), *Towards a Cultural Policy of India*, Vikas, New Delhi, 1974.

4

Capitalism and the Labouring Poor: Victims or Transforming Agents*

I am very grateful to the authorities of the Zakir Husain College of Delhi University for inviting me to deliver this year's Zakir Husain Memorial Lecture. I have chosen the theme of "Capitalism and the Labouring Poor: Some Reflections" for my lecture today. This is a theme which reflects my personal concerns as a sociologist, as a socialist and as a person of an activist temper and orientation for more than four decades of my working life. But this theme was also of very deep concern to Zakir Saheb both as a citizen and a scholar.

It is not known to many that Zakir Saheb worked for his Ph.D. dissertation in Economics at the Berlin University under the supervision of the famous economist and sociologist, Warner Sombart, on the theme "The Agricultural Economy of India". In this dissertation the phenomenon of *capitalism* is explored by examining the Indian economy as an agrarian hinterland of the British Empire. This work was completed in 1928. Much later in 1944-45, Zakir Saheb had occasion again to reflect on the phenomenon of capitalism with all the analytical sophistication of a scholar in a series of ten lectures delivered as Sir Kikabhai Prem Chand Readership lectures. These lectures were published by the Delhi University under the title "Capitalism: An Essay In Understanding" in 1948.

---

* Delivered as Zakir Husain Memorial Lecture at the Zakir Husain College, Delhi University, on February 10, 1992.

Zakir Saheb pursues his enquiry primarily with the aid of the tools and insights provided by Sombart but also incorporates some of the basic ideas and insights of Karl Marx and Max Weber. The questions he asks are of great historical interest but they are also of great contemporary interest, even though the lectures were delivered more than four decades and a half ago. Despite the fact that much has changed since these lectures were delivered, they are still relevant and also very refreshing.

Considering the fact that capitalism, far from becoming obsolescent, is still alive and kicking and that instead of vanishing from the world stage, it has returned to a central position again, the questions posed by Zakir Saheb about the inner resilience and about the prospects of capitalism, specially in the Asian countries, have acquired a new legitimacy and a new relevance. Considering also the fact that so much has been written on capitalism by thinkers, scholars and commentators over such a long period of time, it is a tribute to Zakir Saheb's mental calibre and powers of perception that his lectures still embody perceptions and insights which have proved of enduring value and which continue to have refreshing quality.

As already stated in this essay, Zakir Saheb imaginatively applied the method of thought and the basic insights of his illustrious teacher, Warner Sombart, for an understanding of capitalism. Central to *Sombart's concept of capitalism is the spirit or the economic outlook of capitalism which is the sum total of purposes, motives and principles determining men's behaviour in economic life during a whole epoch*. The economic outlook of capitalism is dominated by three ideas: *acquisition, competition* and *rationality*. And it is these three mutually reinforcing instincts which generated the internal dynamism of capitalism as an economic system as distinguished from previous economic systems which were characterised by slow growth of productive forces. In Sombart's view, as a result of the lack of understanding of the sources of resilience of capitalism economic experiments for finding a substitute for capitalism either failed or did not achieve the desired results. *This was because these experiments, which tried to remove the evils of capitalism also damaged the basic motive forces of growth—viz. principles of acquisition, competition and rationality—which had accounted for the resilience of capitalism.* In a very perceptive and indeed, highly prophetic observation, Sombart remarked how "the Russians grasped less than any other nation the peculiar character of the capitalist economy when they banished the capitalistic enterpreneur and thereby brought the mechanism to a standstill." (Sombart, ibid., p. 205).

Sombart is fully aware that the economic success of capitalism as a productive agent has a sharply negative side. Under capitalism the *economic* side of human life grows and progresses at the cost of the moral and aesthetic side of human life. According to Sombart, the very strength of capitalism becomes its weakness from the perspective of wholesome development of human life. Sombart remarks:

> Wherever acquisition is absolute, the importance of everything else is predicated upon its serviceability to economic interests; a human being is regarded merely as a labour power, nature as an instrument of production, life as one grand commercial transaction, heaven and earth as a large business concern in which everything that lives and moves is registered in a gigantic ledger in terms of its money value. Ideals oriented upon the values of the human personality loosen their hold on man's mind; efforts for the increase of human welfare cease to have any value. Perfection of the business mechanism appears as the only goal worth striving for; the means become an end. (Sombart, ibid., p. 197).

Sombart's analysis is the precursor of Galbraith's more recent insight into the inherent and inexorable logic of the modern techno-structure which excludes all other goals—the educational, cultural, ethical, and aesthetic—except the narrowly economic.

Equally fundamental is Sombart's insight into the contradictory nature of capitalism. Sombart remarks that "while individual action under capitalism is informed by the ideal of the highest rationality, the capitalist system as a whole remains irrational… . From the co-existence of well-nigh perfect rationality and of the greatest irrationality originate the numerous strains and stresses which are peculiarly characteristic of the economic system of capitalism." (Sombart, ibid., p. 108).

Sombart treats capitalism as a dynamic system with new features of internal structure and forms of organisation distinguishing different stages of capitalist evolution. Thus "early capitalism" lasting from the thirteenth to the middle of the eighteenth century is followed by "full capitalism" which closed with the outbreak of the First World War and this in turn is followed by the "late capitalism" which is still continuing. While the basic spirit of capitalism characterised all its phases and explained the essence of it as a distinctive social formation, the systems passed through internal structural changes from phase to phase.

It is important to note that Zakir Saheb's treatment of capitalism is not just cold and logical as Sombart's treatment. In Zakir Saheb's exposition logical rigour and empirical support are blended with an emotive quality which is very marked throughout the exposition. Zakir Saheb's essay combines intellectual quality with a *moral passion* which he shares with all radical analysts of capitalism. But unlike many radical thinkers whose moral passion colours their assessment of the working of capitalism as an economic system and makes them highly subjective in their prognosis, *Zakir Saheb combines a high degree of objectivity about the growth potential of capitalism with a sharp perception of the destructive and brutal side of capitalist development*.

Zakir Saheb's "concept of understanding as a method of social science" implies rigorous investigation and analysis but it also transcends its narrow limits. Comprehending the totality of the system and its inner dynamics is as important as illumination of the specific aspects or dimensions of the working of the system. Understanding also implies encompassing the points of view, the feelings, perceptions, the interests, and indeed, the overall contradictory fortunes and destiny of the classes and masses that are caught in the vortex of epochal social transitions like the emergence and development of capitalism. *Understanding means not only deconstruction but overall reconstruction, not only analysis but synthesis, not only illumination but also overall judgement.* It means seeking truth not merely in abstract terms or statistical categories only, but in terms of the sorrows and sufferings, torments and traumas and the prospects for millions and millions of living and real human beings. The familiar economic categories and tools are not enough for understanding. *Sense of history, imagination and empathy, are as indispensable as analytical and logical rigour for real insight into historical processes and into the great human drama called capitalism.*

Why do we attach a great importance to the methodology of studying capitalism? This is because in recent years an ultra-academic view of capitalism has become fashionable as opposed to "the classical" view. This has amounted almost into a deliberate design to shut out from our view the vital dimensions of the social reality of capitalism as an enormously destructive and dehumanising force and to magnify its contribution to economic growth as reflected in quantitative categories. Such a tendency to shut out from our view the brutal side of capitalism is highly fashionable in the current debate on socialism vs. capitalism, 'planning vs. the market'. In this debate bureaucratic socialism and statist 'planning' are rightly under attack for their evils but now 'capitalism' and 'market' are mystified and the darker side of capitalism and the market failure in achieving social ends are ignored. Understanding of the past, therefore, is not only of historical interest. It is crucial for our present-day perception of policy alternatives and for our choices and options in regard to systems, strategies and policies.

In support of my argument I wish to draw upon the path-breaking work of E.P. Thompson entitled *The Making of the English Working Class*. Sharply focussing on the tendency which I indicated above, Thompson writes:

> To see (capitalism) and the working class in this way is to defend a 'classical' view of the period against the prevalent mood of

> contemporary schools of economic history and sociology. For the territory of Industrial Revolution, which was first staked out and surveyed by Marx, Arnold Toynbee, the Webbs and the Hammonds, now resembles an academic battlefield. At point, after point, the familiar 'catastrophic' view of the period has been disputed. Where it was customary to see the period as one of economic disequilibrium, intense misery and exploitation, political repression and heroic popular agitation, attention is now directed to the rate of economic growth (and the difficulties of take-off into self-sustaining technological reproduction). The enclosure movement is now noted less for its harshness in displacing the village poor, than for its success in feeding a rapidly growing population. The hardships of the period are seen as being due to the dislocations consequent upon the wars, faulty communications, immature banking and exchange, uncertain markets and the trade cycle, rather than to exploitation or cut-throat competition.... Thus the Industrial Revolution, it is argued, was an age, not of catastrophe or acute class conflict and class oppression but of improvement.

This dilution of the "catastrophic" view of capitalism or Industrial Revolution to which Thompson drew attention about three decades ago has become the dominant trend in the academic circles and in the political debate in the present period. The 'anti-catastrophic' view in fact has emerged as a trend dominating social consciousness today. To allow this 'anti-catastrophic' view to go unchallenged is to be a partner in the conspiracy against the labouring poor—the labouring poor who were victims of the very logic of capitalist development in history and who continue to be victims of the inherent logic of capitalist development today.

It is important to note that Zakir Saheb is fully aware of the anti-labouring-poor logic of the process of capitalist development.

In this background Zakir Saheb's exposition poses before scholars major questions relating to the destiny of capitalism: What explains the unprecedented resilience of capitalism as a historically conditioned but evolving form of economic organisation? What explains the fact that capitalism has belied the predictions of its disintegration and collapse through the inexorable logic of its own insoluble internal contradictions?

We reproduce Zakir Saheb's own words below on these aspects which have represented a puzzle and a paradox of great complexity both for experts and for laymen:

> Does it not appear reasonable to suppose that some day capitalism will break its neck in a crash like this? It has been the hope of great minds who have devoted themselves most diligently to the study of capitalism. It is, I am afraid, wishful thinking... .
>
> The three pathological developments which were expected to hasten the end of capitalism—increasing misery of the labouring classes, ever-growing concentration, and (recurrent) crisis do not seem to justify the hope or the fear, as one's attitude of approval or disapproval of capitalism might lead one to say... .
>
> Sombart had in a place recorded the conversation he had with Max Weber about the future of economic life. The question was when the witches sabbath of humanity in the capitalist countries will at last come to an end. Max Weber said, "when the last ton of ore has been smelted with the last ton of coal." This moment may not be very far off. ... But if capitalism has managed to survive Marx's prophecy, it can also survive Max Weber's. Even the end of iron and coal will not find capitalism at the end of its resources. . . . No Max Weber's prophecy can also come true.

From this perspective, Zakir Saheb poses the question of the future of capitalism as follows:

> What, then, is the prognosis? Will this amazing work of human perversity continue unchallenged? That it is the result of perversity we have come to know. The motive force—the greed, the covetousness, the urge to acquisition, to untrammelled and unlimited expansion, to unconditional and inconsiderate acquisition—is a perversity. The astonishing thing is that this motive which really has hardly anything to do with natural economic activity has applied itself to economic life and reshaped it from the very foundations. Under the urge of this profit motive an economic structure has come into being so big, so widespread, so mighty, that one stands and gapes and is inclined to mistake its

> bigness for greatness. Starting from almost a scratch an economic system has been built up under which population has increased by a few hundred million; the length of life has increased, exit permits are obtainable with increasing difficulty; the standard of living has been raised under which it has been possible to feed, clothe and house a much larger number of people than ever before in human history—and yes, to amuse them evening after evening; under which life has been changed beyond recognition; under which the wonders of technique have come to pass, empires have risen and fallen, under which men have toiled as never before and not known the joy of work, under which men have earned as never before and not known even to relate their earnings with their lives, under which means have become ends, and absolute aims and ends and values been forgotten.

In his prognosis for European capitalism in its phase of "late capitalism" Zakir Saheb takes note, as Sombart did, not only of the important changes concerning the internal structure of capitalism but also of changes imposed on capitalism by the growth of "the social conscience". It is "social conscience" which makes society assume the upper hand and forces capitalism to subordinate itself to social purpose; it is "social conscience" which makes society take over very extensive and ever-growing fields of economic activity from the capitalist entrepreneur and to organise it as a "planned social economy" even in the strongholds of capitalism.

Zakir Saheb in this way shows that the growth of the "social conscience" and of society's ever-growing capability to curb the "overall irrationality" (a la Sombart) of capitalism and to make it conform to society's will were major factors due to which Marx's prediction was proved wrong. This implies that it is not Marx, the economist, formulating the law of mass immiserisation as a basic tendency of capitalism who proved wrong. It was Marx, the political scientist, who proved wrong by not fully appreciating the prospects of growing "social conscience" specially in a democracy and its capacity to check if not subvert the basic economic tendency of capitalism.

But Zakir Saheb as a discerning analyst takes full account of the *long interval* between the emergence of the trends of mass "pauperism" and immiserisation and the growth of "a social conscience" (or, to use Galbraith's phrase, counter-veiling power) capable of counter-acting these trends. And it is "this long interval" during which there was neither any remedy nor was their any social protest which is shut out from our view by apologists of capitalism. It is "this long interval" which was a matter of deep concern and reflection for Zakir Saheb. In other words, if the phenomenon of misery and exploitation emerged on the surface as a pervasive evil during "early capitalism", the consciousness of it appeared only in the phase of "full-grown capitalism" and the remedy for it emerged largely in the phase of "the late capitalism". And in some sense misery and exploitation have not totally disappeared even now in the developed world.

If this is the way how capitalism could escape Marx's prophecy of its downfall, how did it escape Max Weber's prophecy? It can be said from hindsight that Max Weber, perhaps like Malthus in a different context, had a very static view of resources required by capitalism and he underestimated the possibilities of scientific progress and of the discovery of new resources and new sources of energy which gave capitalism a newer and newer lease of life.

Even in regard to resources, however, one must not ignore the highly destructive implications of the way the greed and covetousness of capitalism has led it to seek, exploit, over-exploit the natural resources of the world; how the recklessness of capitalism has caused enormous damage to ecology and environment and ultimately, to the inherent balance and harmony of the natural system. And, above all, one must not overlook how by creating an antagonistic relationship between man and nature, capitalism damaged the original vision of harmony between men and nature, without which there can be no long-term prospect of a viable and enduring human civilisation. Did Marx not cherish the goal of 'humanising nature and of naturalising man' as the cornerstone of a humanist socialist vision? And, according to him, damaging the harmony of man and nature was the major sin of which capitalism had to be regarded as guilty.

And here again between the 'growing phase of capitalism' characterised by massive damage to nature and to the natural resource system and the period of 'late capitalism' which is characterised by the consciousness of this damage and the introduction of corrective mechanisms for checking damage to ecology and environment and restoring the health of the natural system, there is a long historical interval, a period of darkness as it were, before a glimmer of light is seen on the horizon.

Here again one should be quick to point out that it is not as if that "the social conscience" once aroused will always remain active and alert. Human beings, as Myrdal pointed out long ago, have a tendency to relapse into a state of moral apathy or "moral discord" and to rationalise their apathy on the basis of some ethical principle or the other.

In recent years there has again been a deadening of the "social conscience" which has been aided by a new economic philosophy which deplores public action and government intervention in favour of the unfortunate and disadvantaged in society. Drawing attention to this, J.K. Galbraith observed in a speech at the University of California in 1980 as follows:

> My first plea is for a strong revival of what anciently has been called the social ethic, what more simply is a good sense of the community. This is not a subtle or a sophisticated thing; it is the will, in an increasingly interdependent world, to be concerned with what one must do jointly with others, to have as much pride in this achievement, as one has in what does for oneself.
>
> In the last few years we have witnessed the growth of a contrary mood, and nowhere more manifestly than here in California. This is the celebration, even the sanctification of self-concern. A person's highest duty, it is held, is to his own income, his own personal enjoyment; freedom is the freedom to get money with the minimum of constraint and to spend it with the smallest possible contribution to public purposes. So defined, freedom is purely a first person affair. No attention may be given to public

> action that enhances the freedom of someone else. In accordance with first-person ethic, deduction from private income for public schools, hospitals, playgrounds, libraries or public assistance to the disadvantaged or the poor means a net loss of liberty....
>
> Partly it is unwise to be too specific, the new concern for self regularly takes the form of an attack on government in the abstract. Government and the associated bureaucracy are proclaimed the great and faceless enemies of personal freedom. This avoids mention of the many good things that the government does for all, including the self concerned. And there is a further advantage in so disguising things; those involved do not wish it thought that this new preoccupation with self is a revolt of the rich against the poor. When so identified, it loses some of its appeal. For some crusades there must be a decent camouflage.
>
> We should not be misled.... The everyday public services are most used by the poor. The affluent can have private education; the poor must have public schools. The very affluent if they are indeed very affluent can buy books; poorer children need a public library. It is the poor who frequent the public playgrounds and the public hospitals. Welfare payments have a particular beneficence for the man or woman or family who has no other income.
>
> Messers Howard Jarvis and Milton Freedman heading this new crusade for the self do not, of course, present themselves as enemies of the poor. They are friends of freedom and enemies of government. But no one should be in doubt about the object of their crusade; it is against the least fortunate of our citizens.

Galbraith goes further and comments on the implications of this revolt against the poor for the viability of capitalism. His remarks given below are very penetrating:

> There are consequences of this revolt against the poor that should be of special concern to conservatives. Capitalism did not survive in the United States or in other industrial countries because of a rigid adherence to individualist precept—the sacrifice of those who could not make it in a stern, competitive struggle. It survived because of a continuing and generally a successful effort to soften its sharp edges—to minimise the suffering and discontent of those who fail in face of competition, economic power, ethnic disadvantage, or

> moral, mental or physical incapacity. It was this ability of modern industrial society to develop and, on occasion, to enforce a sense of community that Marx failed to foresee.

I have quoted these long passages from Galbraith with a twofold aim. First, I wish to reinforce the point that I made earlier that *social forces have been activated within developed industrial societies which have somewhat curbed and softened the inhuman face of capitalism and made it compatible with a certain degree of concern for the welfare of the disadvantaged and the deprived.* Second, Galbraith's remarks also reveal how the fundamental spirit of capitalism is oriented primarily to concern for the self and the disregard for non-self and this exclusive concern for the self has a tendency to assert itself into prominence again and again and to prevail over "social conscience" or the regard for the non-self.

A new philosophical wind favouring self at the expense of the non-self which is blowing in the Western world has also begun to invade the non-Western world.

It must be recognised that the failure of the non-capitalist economic models to serve as viable models of growth and as effective substitutes of capitalism have made Asian countries like India vulnerable to the individualistic winds from the West. Socialists must recognise that celebration of the failure of the socialist model has also begun to mean the celebration of a new future for capitalism in India, that is, in one of the largest countries of the world.

It is in this background that one must *take note of the prognosis regarding the strong possibilities of an Asian capitalism that Zakir Saheb had made four and a half decades ago*. His words have proved to be as prophetic as they were perceptive. It is obvious now that radicals had not seriously reckoned with the potentialities of an Asian capitalism and of capitalism striking deeper roots in the Asian soil. From this angle Zakir Saheb had a better appreciation of the Indian realities than many others. It is also obvious that while Zakir Saheb found it very hard emotionally to reconcile himself to this prospect, he did not shrink intellectually from the logic of his own enquiry of his into recognising this strong tendency.

To quote:

> Since I have allowed myself to be drawn into the rather uncertain domain of prophecy I may as well say that *the stage seems to be set for the growth of an Asiatic capitalism* in which India appears marked for a big role; that this new capitalism, although it will have its distinct individuality, will not be very much different from its Western predecessor can be easily assumed. The forces that can be expected to range themselves against it will, I feel, not be strong enough to stop the new growth. They themselves have not the courage, the imagination, and the experience to put the Indian economy on a higher level of efficiency. The capitalist seems to me to have more of these and he seems resolved to try himself. He is apparently ready to subject himself to state control and regulation; should we be surprised if he is also planning to control and regulate the state? No, I do not think the Asiatic and Indian capitalism will be much different from the Western.
>
> May be that it has less of the conquerer in it to begin with, but oh, it will have an inexhaustible fund of what we called the civic virtues at its disposal; the clever calculator, the shrewd diplomat will compensate for the lack of bellicose bravado. If it is not given to him, for a while, to get the riches that come from power, he will exercise the power that comes from riches. *We seem fated to go through the whole gamut*. Capitalism will set up the machinery, the apparatus of our economic life for his gain, and when he has run the mad race, *the social conscience will assert itself*, but will do so successfully only when the chances of maintaining economic life at a high level are assured and change the private profit economy of capitalism into the planned social economy for satisfying needs. *How long, oh, how long, and then to imagine what must fill the interval*.

As raised by Zakir Saheb long ago, the relevant question even today is: *are we condemned to live with capitalism and with the harsh logic of all that early capitalism brings in its wake?* To this question there is no easy answer because the answer does not lie entirely in the realm of economics but also in the realm of society's consciousness, perceptions and choices and, above all, in the realm of the level of organisation and consciousness of the labouring poor, who will be called upon to pay the price for untrammelled capitalist growth.

In making his prognosis Zakir Saheb took mostly economics into account and not emerging socio-political processes and forces. The source of complexities in the social situation of latecomer and Asian countries like India is that *here a strong anti-capitalist consciousness has already taken deep roots—much, much before capitalism could complete the tasks of modern economic development*. In other words, a "social conscience" has already emerged as a factor to reckon with before capitalist economic transition has been effected. There is, therefore, no question of tolerating "a long interval" between completion of the economic transition and the rise of a "social conscience" as in Western economic history which was noted by Zakir Saheb. *In India the rise of a "social conscience" has preceded a capitalist breakthrough.*

The fact that the awakening of the poor can block a smooth capitalist transition if the interests of the poor are disregarded is a major factor to reckon with. But the fact that any viable alternative to capitalism is not in sight and that the image of socialism has already been darkened by the collapse of the Second World and the failure of bureaucratic state socialism within the country can also not be disregarded. Does it mean then a social stalemate? I am not inclined to surrender my faith that the ultimate answer lies with the labouring poor. That in the new era they are not condemned to be passive and helpless victims of a capitalist transition as in the past. They are destined to be transforming agents of a "just society".

5

Socialism: A Lost Cause or A Long Revolution?

In his *Communist Manifesto* in 1847 Karl Marx had, with his penetrating scientific outlook and indomitable daring of a revo-lutionary, made the historic declaration that a "spectre is haunting Europe, the spectre of Communism!" At the same time, in an inspiring call to the workers of the world he had declared that their future was tied up with communism and to realise the dream of a communist society was their historic mission and responsibility. This message of Karl Marx gave a new turn to human history not only in Europe but throughout the world. "Workers of the world unite, you have nothing to lose but your chains!" This became the battle cry of the working people the world over.

However, the process of the socialist revolution Marx had predicted did not begin from those European countries where capitalism had struck deep roots and had been instrumental in giving a tremendous boost to productive forces. It started from a very backward country, Russia, where the reverse was true. The Russian economy was stagnant and crisis-ridden not because capitalism there had attained high peaks of growth, but because capitalism's growth was extremely slow and stunted and had been thwarted by powerful internal constraints. As Marx had not even imagined, the factors that created a revolutionary situation in that country were not related to internal contradictions of a highly developed capitalism, but, on the contrary, were the product of an undeveloped or underdeveloped capitalism, as Lenin had understood them to be. Russia in 1917 thus had represented an unbalanced economy with stunted capitalist growth, and the process of revolutions which began from Russia had later engulfed the whole of Eastern Europe. And then it became a revolutionary wave sweeping the backward landmasses of Asia, Africa and Latin America.

It needs to be remembered that the October Revolution in Russia and the socialist revolutions that followed in Eastern Europe had been led by parties subscribing to the communist philosophy, to Marxism-Leninism. But these revolutions had also received widespread support from several eminent liberal intellectuals and thinkers who, although committed basically to liberal democratic philosophy and its essentially humanistic ethos and values, were also deeply concerned about the sharpening internal contradictions of the capitalist system and their disorienting and degrading economic, cultural and social consequences. They had a hope that socialism would help revive and eventually contribute to the realisation of the humanistic, egalitarian and anti-exploitation ideals and social objectives of radical liberalism, which capitalism had discarded and undermined.

Thus, not all the acknowledged intellectuals of the world who had supported the economic and social experiments of the Soviet state from its very first years subscribed to the communist ideology. Some of them like Romain Rolland, George Bernard Shaw, Red Dean of Canterbury, H.G. Wells, Rabindranath Tagore, John Maynard Keynes and Jawaharlal Nehru were even sharply critical of certain ingredients of this ideology, e.g. its support to authoritarianism and to violence as a means of social transformation. If they still welcomed these Soviet experiments it was because they perceived as their mainspring the humanistic values and ideals radical liberalism had basically represented when it had emerged on the scene. It was as an opponent of the oppressive social system and anti-egalitarian way of thinking of the Middle Ages that liberalism had emerged as a historic force in human history, but these very ideals it had later discarded. This was conceded even by a liberal economist like Gunnar Myrdal who had characterised Western civilisation as a civilisation caught in "a moral discord"—professing ideals in words which were repudiated in actual practice. Communism, by upholding and adopting these ideals, disowned and discarded in practice by the West, had received acclaim and support of the eminent intellectuals all over the world who had been disillusioned by the moral discord of liberalism and who had seen in Russian socialism a new hope for mankind.

We are now confronted with a riddle of history indeed. Russian socialism had emerged as the harbinger of freedom from the deadening remnants of oppressive feudalism and from the internal contradictions and crippling constraints of decadent capitalism. It had taken the lead in reviving and realising the basic values of the Western renaissance, especially its stress on equality and brotherhood that capitalism had forgotten. For several reasons, however, Russian socialism had become a victim of its own internal contradictions and tensions and of the selfishness, lust for power and corruption of its new ruling class. It had cut itself off from its basic inspirations and ideals, and after seven decades of the October Revolution history had taken a turn towards severe opposition of the Communist system from working people as well as thoughtful intellectuals.

A century and a half after the launching of the Communist Manifesto and totally contrary to Karl Marx's prophecy, a new spectre is spreading all over the globe, "the spectre of anti-communism". First, the economic system of the East European countries, which was claimed to have been inspired by the Communist philosophy, and the political regime buttressing this system, could not withstand the storm of people's revolt and collapsed like a house of cards. Within a few months, the Communist system of the world's Second Great Power and Communism's strongest citadel, Russia, and other constituents of the Soviet Union, which had taken seven decades to build up also collapsed and vanished from the world map.

It was the Soviet Union's own acknowledged leader, Mikhail Gorbachev, who had said that history had proved that *the communist experiment which Lenin had started after the October Revolution was a failed project.* In a sense, it was the series of revolutions after the First and Second World Wars which had given birth to the Second World of socialism as a rival of capitalism's citadel, the First World; but this Second World had virtually disappeared from Eastern Europe and Soviet Russia. A number of Western scholars now expect China's communist system to meet the same fate, the setting of the sun of communism in its totality.

Those who had always been against communism now openly and gleefully declare that they had always predicted this fate for a system representing an Evil Empire a la Reagan; that the system which brutally suppressed individual liberty and private enterprise would be wiped out completely. But even those who were not or are not against communism are worried at this turn of events and are tormented by the question *whether in the battle between capitalism and socialism the former has indeed emerged the victor and the latter the vanquished.* Ruling classes and intellectuals of neutral nations like India which till recently had seen their future in the socialist direction, have now decisively made a break from socialist ideology and 'socialist pattern of society' and have turned towards capitalism in which alone they seem to have faith and confidence for their growth and development.

Today, countries in Asia, Africa and Latin America, where the intelligentsia had reposed confidence in some form of socialism, have forsaken the "unsuccessful" path associated with this creed and are again centring their attention on capitalism like prodigal sons. *Why did this happen is a question agitating the minds of all thinking people.* But is a dispassionate inquiry into this question possible in the present surcharged atmosphere in the world in which a universal frenzy of anti-communism has made an independent, unbiased consideration of the issue difficult, if not impossible?

The aberrations and distortions of what is described as the communist system have been exposed in all their nakedness to the world, and those who read newspapers are very familiar with them. A large section of the common people, too, has come to know of them through the electronic media. In fact, the media has not only given wide publicity to these distortions of the communist system, but it has also been presenting a highly exaggerated and prettified image of capitalism, and if it is to be believed, there is only one key to solve the economic crisis caused by socialism, namely, restoration of capitalism and unfettered freedom for expansion of a free capitalist market. It is noteworthy that among the new missionaries and crusaders for "this free market capitalism" we have in the front rank not just the ideologues of the Western world championing the cause of capitalism in the name of "neo-liberalism" and "new economic reforms", for instance, the international agencies like the World Bank and the International Monetary Fund. *What is most tragic is that among these front rank patrons and promoters of "neo-liberalism" are also former high ranking Marxists-Leninists like Boris Yeltsin who after his first visit to the United States returned to his country almost hypnotised, specially, by America's affluence and its consumerist ethos in contrast to the situation in his home country.* In his well-publicised book *Against the Grain—An Autobiography*, Yeltsin summed up his impressions of America in the following words:

> A great deal has been written on my trip to America.... I met with many interesting people from President Bush to ordinary Americans on the streets of their eleven cities. No doubt, it will sound banal but what surprised me most were precisely those ordinary people in America who radiated optimism and faith in themselves and in their country. There were, of course, shattering experiences of another sort—*the supermarkets for example.* When I saw those shelves crammed with hundreds, thousands of cans, cartons, and goods of every possible sort, for the first time I felt quite frankly sick with despair for the Soviet people—that such a potentially super rich country as ours has been brought to a state of such poverty! It is terrible to think of it. (Boris Yeltsin, 1990: 255).

The contrast between the overall American affluence and Russian "scarcity", no doubt, would have struck any superficial observer comparing the two systems and two situations. But Yeltsin did not have time to explore deeper and to take cognizance of the marked contrast between the economic and social security offered to the people below by the Soviet system and the total insecurity and homelessness to which the "underclass" of the American cities was subjected under the American system which had everything to offer but only to those with "effective demand" but not to those with needs but no resources to satisfy them.

One wonders whether Boris Yeltsin has even reflected on the devastating and shattering impact of the "market-driven economic reforms" which were introduced in Russia under his leadership on the Russian people at large, specially the rural and urban poor who have been driven to total economic insecurity and, under its pressure, to economic deprivation and beggary and even to crimes unheard of before under the Soviet system. It is established beyond doubt that the dismantling of the "command economy" and the introduction of the "market economy" did not create in Yeltsin's Russia the pre-conditions of American type "affluence". It only drove Russia into deeper and deeper economic malaise.

In the concluding part of his autobiography, Boris Yeltsin had characterised his country "as the only country left on the earth which is trying to enter the twenty-first century with an obsolete nineteenth century ideology, that we are the last inhabitants of a country defeated by socialism, as one clever man put it." (Boris Yeltsin, 1990: 262).

It was Boris Yeltsin's dream and his ambition to pull Russia out of its domination by an anachronistic and obsolete nineteenth century ideology and to set it on the path of entry into the twenty-first century by adopting the neo-liberalism of the Western neo-capitalist ideologues. At the time of his departure from the Russian political scene Yeltsin seems to have succeeded not in giving Russia a push towards "liberal democracy" and the release of new productive forces under the capitalist restoration; *he seems to have succeeded in creating a backlash towards a growing ultra-nationalistic authoritarianism and a fast spreading economic chaos, and anarchy*. The resurgence of "crony capitalism" under which the elite accumulates and accumulates ill-gotten wealth and the masses are entrapped in a vicious circle of scarcity, insecurity and unemployment—that is what drive towards new liberalism has given to Russia "liberated from the tyranny of Stalinist socialism".

To return to our main question: "Does the end of Stalinist socialism or the Second World signify also the end of the dreams which had motivated and inspired this great experiment in designing a new economic system free from the anarchy and chaos and degradation of capitalism? Does the end of the Second World also signify the final victory of the First World and its ideology? In a situation when even to imagine of socialism has become impossible, and, in the vacuum created by its downfall a strenuous attempt is being made to bring back capitalism, the question also inevitably arises: *what does this much sought after post-modern capitalism really signify?*"

In my view, the crisis confronting mankind today is not confined to the erstwhile socialist camp; it is equally deep in the camp of liberal capitalism, indeed in its very citadels in the West. Hence, it will be more appropriate to call it a universal crisis of economic systems. It is the persistent attempt of the Western media and short-sighted elements among Western intelligentsia to divert even the little attention that was centred on the internal crisis of liberal capitalism to the crisis of the Second and Third World systems alone, especially from the point when following Eastern Europe, the Soviet Union, too, had became its victim. Taking advantage of this situation not only has the focus been shifted away from the crisis of post-modern capitalism, but by presenting it as a crisis-free system its "achievements" have been projected as a miracle. The new generation's disillusionment with the Second and Third World experiments in socialism has, in fact, been exploited to make the people fall for new capitalism. The media and the self-serving elements have undoubtedly attained considerable success in this attempt.

In this new background it is necessary to emphasise once again that the present crisis of the human condition is a worldwide crisis as not only the distinguished European and American intellectuals and old Marxists, Paul Baran and C. Wright Mills, but thoughtful economists like J.K. Galbraith, radical thinkers like Noam Chomsky and other liberal intellectuals of the contemporary world have also acknowledged. If the Marxist-communist philosophy culminated in the Stalinist thought system, an inhuman dictatorship and an economy of scarcity, the liberal philosophy, too, has had its culmination in individualistic, self-serving consumerism and unbridled hedonism and emergence of what Myrdal once called the horrifying expansion of the 'industrial-military and academic' complex. The vast ramifications of this complex have destroyed the balance in the relationships between man and nature, man and man and man and woman, and have posed a serious threat to the security of both nature and human beings and their life sources. In fact, the new capitalist system has created a terrible vicious circle of instrumentation by turning man into a mere machine. As a result, the basic humanistic values and inspirations of the European renaissance which had enabled capitalism to capture power from feudalism, have virtually become extinct in today's post-modern capitalist age, and this once progressive system, in its new incarnation of unbridled consumerism, has crossed all limits of restraint, self-discipline and self-limitation without which no civilisation and culture can remain viable, vigorous and stable.

This 'consumerist capitalism' has brought entire mankind to the brink of insecurity and disaster caused by sapping its internal vitality. Through commercialisation of the sacred man-woman relationship it has sacrificed woman at the altar of hedonism and limitless voluptuousness and self-indulgence. If we look deeply we will find that together with the erstwhile Second World's own internal malaise, surreptitious infiltration of the consumerist tendencies of the West into the communist world had also played no mean role in destabilising and weakening the social outlook and cultural values which had sustained socialism at its roots. *What even unfailing military weapons could not achieve, the glamour and mirage of consumerism did by diverting the minds and hearts of the Soviet ruling class and citizens away from the basic socialist ideals and values.* Therefore, among the main causes of the decline and disintegration of the Soviet Union, the volcanic eruption of self-indulgence and indiscriminate pursuit of the pleasure principle was also a vastly destabilising force. *With this explosion of consumerism, the basic moral distinction between communism and capitalism in which communism's moral superiority had its source became extinct.*

It is a matter of great concern that the people in a large segment of the world who till now had not regarded consumerism as the motivating force and their life's philosophy have now started according recognition and legitimacy to it and thereby given a tremendous boost to world capitalism. This development cannot be considered as merely an internal crisis of Russia and Eastern Europe. It is a crisis of the human civilisation as a whole and a matter of serious concern for the intelligentsia of the entire world. We can realise what a great tragedy this development represents only when we remember that despite the many serious shortcomings, distortions and aberrations of the Soviet system, *several thinkers and seers during the early years of this system had seen in it possibilities of an alternative to the barbarism of capitalism and had also looked upon the socialist experiments as a challenge to the tendency underlying capitalism that regarded human beings as mere animals driven by greed and avarice.* In this context, the statement of the reputed British economist, John Maynard Keynes, in his "A Short View of Russia" written after his trip to the Soviet Union in 1925, is extremely relevant. This statement of Keynes, in which he had referred to the possibilities of the Soviet system, is also significant because of his established image as a saviour or deliverer of capitalism from its internal crisis. Commenting on the larger significance of the Soviet experiment for entire mankind, Keynes remarked:

> At any rate to me it seems clearer every day that the moral problem of our age is concerned with the love of money, with the habitual appeal to the money motive in nine-tenths of the activities of life, with the universal striving after individual economic security as the prime object of endeavour, with the social approbation of money as the measure of constructive success, and with the social appeal to the hoarding instinct as the foundation of the necessary provision for the family and for the future. The decaying religions around us, which have less and less interest for most people unless it be as an agreeable form of magical, ceremonial or of social observance, have lost their moral significance just because—unlike some of their earlier versions—they do not touch in the least degree on their essential matters. *A revolution in our ways of thinking and feeling about money may become the growing purpose of contemporary embodiments of the ideal. Perhaps, therefore, Russian communism does represent the first confused stirrings of a great religion.*

Elaborating further this basic insight into the Soviet system, Keynes observed:

> Here (in Soviet Russia), one feels at moments, in spite of poverty, stupidity and oppression, is the laboratory of life. Here the chemicals are being mixed in new combination, and stink and explode. Something—there is just a chance— might come out. And even a chance gives to what is happening in Russia more importance than what is happening (let us say) in the United States of America....
>
> But if Russia is going to be a force in the outside world it will not be the result of Mr. Zinovieff's money. Russia will never matter seriously to the rest of us, unless it be as a moral force. So, now the deeds are done and there is no going back, I shall like to give Russia her chance; to help and not to hinder. For now much rather, even after allowing for everything, if I were a Russian would I contribute my quota of activity to Soviet Russia than to Tsarist Russia! I could not subscribe to the new official faith any more than to the old. I should detest the actions of the new tyrants not less than those of the old. But I should feel that my eyes were turned towards and no longer away from the possibilities of things; that out of the cruelty and stupidity of old Russia nothing could ever emerge, but that

beneath the cruelty and stupidity of the new Russia some speck of the ideals may lie hid.

Further clarifying his statement, Keynes had thrown more light on this constructive aspect of Russian communism in the following words:

> I do not mean that Russian communism alters or even seeks to alter, human nature, that it makes Jews less avaricious or Russians less extravagant than they were before. I do not merely mean that it sets up a new ideal. *I mean that it tries to construct a framework of society in which pecuniary motives as influencing action shall have a changed relative importance,* in which social approbations shall be differently distributed, and where behaviours, which previously was normal and respectable, ceases to be either the one or the other" (John Maynard Keynes, "A Short View of Russia",— Nation and Athenaeum -10,17 and 23 October 1925, later included in Keynes's "Essays in Persuasion (Chapter 1,3).

Evidently, an economist and seer of Keynes's stature had given his moral and intellectual support to Russian Communism because in the impulses that motivated it he had seen new possibilities of man's freedom from greed for money. He had said that in spite of its great achievements it was a curse of capitalism that the motivation behind all its achievements was man's excessive greed for money, and while this has certainly enabled the capitalist system to make a gigantic contribution to material progress it has had to pay a heavy price for it in the decline of the moral and spiritual values this progress had entailed. In the Communist experiment in Russia Keynes had seen the dream of material prosperity within the disciplinary framework and predominance of non-material, non-pecuniary, moral values.

The uniqueness of the Russian communist experiment had also moved Rabindranath Tagore. In his "Letters from Russia", Tagore wrote:

> We must admit that to come to visit Russia at my age and my present state of health was a rash undertaking. But since I had

> received the invitation, it would have been unpardonable not to see the light of this mightiest sacrificial fire that has been lit in the world's history.

In this background we can appreciate how the failure of the Russian communist experiment in a sense is a terrible tragedy for mankind. What it signifies is the failure of a historic experiment to find a new morally inspiring force for human progress, to find an alternative to human beings' excessive and immoral greed for money. *But the moral problem mankind was faced with for whose solution Keynes had seen possibilities in the Russian experiment and, therefore, had given it his support, remains.* According to a number of thinkers, a situation of scarcity makes man greedy, and as he advances towards prosperity, it gives place to more liberal and nobler instincts. But the reality is just the opposite. As man becomes more prosperous his greed also increases. Particularly in the developed countries, the economic system, by keeping money in a pivotal position, keeps man's creative capabilities centred only on its augmentation. And by giving primacy to hedonism and utilitarianism, it continuously neglects in practice the principle of beauty and also the nurturing of the non-material side of human nature. Reputed American economist, J.K. Galbraith, in his book *The New Industrial State*, has eloquently emphasised this point. Let us see how he describes this aspect of the economic system of prosperous nations. He makes the following comment on the primacy given to money and on neglect of the activities which make living beautiful and aesthetic:

> No other social goal is more strongly avowed than economic growth. No other test of social success has such nearly unanimous acceptance as the annual increase in the Gross National Product.... The acceptance of economic growth as a social goal coincides closely with the rise to power of the mature corporations and the technostructure. And the latter has had every reason to value it as a social goal. It does not argue the merits of this goal. As always it proceeds by massive assumption. What other goal could be socially so urgent? (J.K. Galbraith, 1967:173 and 175).

Equally significant is Galbraith's statement that the intrinsic drive of the industrial system does not inspire man to strive to make his life beautiful and elegant, but, on the other hand, suppresses this urge. To quote Galbraith again:

> The aesthetic experience was once a very large part of life—unimaginably large, given the resources of earlier societies and values of the modern industrial system. The traveller from the United States or the industrial cities of Europe or Japan goes each summer to visit the remnants of pre-industrial civilisations. That is because Athens, Florence, Venice, Seville, Agra, Kyoto and Samarkand though they were infinitely poor by the standards of modern Nagoya, Dusseldurf, Deganham, Flint or Magnitogorsk, included, as part of life, a much wider aesthetic perspective. No city of the post-industrial era is, in consequence, of remotely comparable artistic interest. Indeed no traveller of predominantly artistic interest ever visits an industrial city and visits very few of any kind which owe their distinction to architecture and urban design postdating the publication of Adam Smith's *Wealth of Nations* in 1776.

Further:

> One of the terms of disapprobation in the industrial system is aesthete. This is because aesthetic achievement is beyond the reach of the industrial system and, in substantial measure, in conflict with it. There would be little need to stress the conflict were it not part of the litany of the industrial system that none exists.
>
> The conflict derives partly from a conflict in goals and partly because aesthetic goals are beyond the reach of the technostructure, which is to say that it cannot identify itself with them. So if they are strongly asserted they will be viewed as a constraint. (Ibid., p. 349).

Remember, the socialist system emerging from the October Revolution had striven to bring the question of culture from the margin to the centre, and because of this commitment had attached great importance to making people's life aesthetic and beautiful even in a situation of poverty. Construction of theatres in every state, town and region, making literary classics available to people at affordable prices, production of low priced records of Western classical music of great masters like Beethoven, Mozart, Bach, etc., are some of the examples of this great effort of the Russian socialist system in the sphere of culture, testifying to its sensitivity and commitment to people's cultural advancement. Later, its mad race for economic development with capitalism drove it to a course which, while leaving this development a mere mirage, gave a body blow to these initial efforts to make life more beautiful.

Jawaharlal Nehru, too, had taken a positive view of this initial thrust of Russian communism on humanistic, non-material advancement of the people, albeit with some reservations about the means it had adopted in pursuit of its objectives. He had said:

> I have the greatest admiration for many of the achievements of the Soviet Union. Among these great achievements is the value attached to the child and the common man. Their systems of education and health are probably the best in the world. But it is said, and rightly, that there is suppression of individual freedom there. And yet the spread of education in all is itself a tremendous liberating force which ultimately will not tolerate that suppression of freedom. This again is another contradiction. Unfortunately, communism became too closely associated with the necessity for violence and thus the idea which it placed before the world became a tainted one. Means distorted ends. We see here the powerful influence of wrong means and methods.

Taking a comparative view of communism and capitalism, Nehru had posed the question of going beyond them and looking for a more satisfactory alternative. To quote:

> Communism charges the capitalist structure of society with being based on violence and class conflict. I think this is essentially correct, though that capitalist structure itself has undergone and is continually undergoing a change because of democratic and other struggles against inequality. The question is how to get rid of this and have a classless society with equal opportunities for all. Can this be achieved only through methods of violence, or is it possible to bring about those changes, through peaceful methods?

> Communism has definitely allied itself to the approach of violence.... It does not seek to change by persuasion or peaceful democratic pressures, but by coercion and indeed by destruction and extermination.... This is completely opposed to the peaceful approach which Gandhiji taught us. (Jawaharlal Nehru, "The Basic Approach", August 15, 1958).

In this context we have to give serious thought to the cultural consequences of the failure of the socialist experiment and re-establishment of capitalism and free market as the dominant economic system all over the world. The questions that arise in this new situation are, no doubt, important for the world community as a whole, but they are even more so for Asian countries like India, China and others. We should not forget that the repercussions of the retreat of socialism on the world plane are not confined to Eastern Europe and Russia. Mao's China and Nehru's India that were exploring alternatives to capitalism in their specific ways have also been severely affected by it. If this non-capitalist experiment has also failed, as is being widely claimed, then towards which new experiment is India setting its course? *Is this new experiment pushing us into the camp of free marketism?* If this is true, what will happen to the socialist ideals and objectives which were associated with the Nehruvian socialist experiment and for whose realisation this experiment was designed as an instrument? In giving up this experiment are we giving up these ideals and objectives as well?

Jawaharlal Nehru himself, in talking about the search for a Third Course between Western capitalism and Russian Stalinism, had only this basic consideration in mind: *how to reconcile and harmonise the objective of improving material conditions of the poor through economic development and that of making their life civilized, aesthetic and beautiful.* He had emphatically said that in giving primacy to creation of wealth and neglecting other, non-material aspects of life, Western capitalism had given rise to terrible imbalances and distortions and after following this skewed course for centuries, had to think in terms of overcoming them through conceptualisation of a democratic and welfare state.

In Russia, too, the non-pecuniary motivation of its communism died after Lenin's demise, and Stalinism which became the reigning philosophy, adopted a contrary course.

When India became independent and national reconstruction became the principal national objective, Nehru had raised the question of the path this national reconstruction should take. Shall we adopt the capitalist model of the Western countries or take up the Russian socialist model, or work out some other new course to suit our conditions, he had asked. Speaking at a meeting of the Standing Committee of the National Development Council on the "Concept of Long-term Planning" in New Delhi on January 7, 1956, Nehru said:

> I am not prepared in the least to copy either Russia or America because both may be, from India's viewpoint, utterly and absolutely wrong. Both may succeed in a narrow plane, and they have succeeded, for example, in reaching a very high standard of material comfort. America has succeeded and Russia, no doubt, will also succeed, provided America and Russia do not collapse before that through war. But we need not regard as inevitable all the other things that happened to these highly industrialised countries where they achieved material advancement. We have seen that they have led them in a direction which may ultimately bring about ruin in spite of the high state of civilisation that they have produced.

In exploring an alternative to the communist system for which Nehru had expressed great admiration in his major work *The Discovery of India* in 1945, Nehru did not regress into supporting capitalism or neo-capitalism which was current in the new citadel of Western capitalism, the United States of America. Nehru was unambiguous and unqualified in his observation that "capitalism and the type of the society it brought about have had their day even though capitalism even in its original home England, was different from what it was in the nineteenth century." Nehru, therefore, in the light of historical experience had posed the following question as extremely relevant for India:

> Should we in India go through the same old process (of building capitalism) and then reverse it? We have the choice before us and we have the experience of others. Why not take the benefits of the higher technological and industrial experience without necessarily getting the wrong consequence which will create difficulties and cause internal and external conflicts? (Jawaharlal Nehru's *Speeches*, Vol. Ill, 1957, pp. 77-78).

It is to this course that Nehru had given the name of the "Third Way". And it is the quest for this balance that had marked the social and economic objectives of the Nehruvian experiment. It is the absence of this balanced approach that had not only distorted socialism but had also damaged post-modern capitalism. It can be said in passing that Nehru's successors in their impatience to find quick solutions, *are discarding not only the prescriptions of the Nehru era but also Jawaharlal Nehru's basic concerns, ideals and approach.* They are discarding the very concept of going beyond Western capitalism and Russian communism in search of a "Third Way".

It is true that every age raises new problems, new challenges before itself. But on how the thinkers of that age define and understand these questions and challenges will depend their success or failure in finding historically correct and viable answers to these questions and ways to meet these challenges. Our understanding of the reasons for the failure of the socialist experiment on the world plane is likewise inextricably linked with our quest for new thinking and new directions to solve the problems and meet the challenges confronting us in the new era.

The basic issue facing socialist intellectuals all over the world following the collapse of the Second World and the disintegration of the Third World is: should socialism be treated as a flawed philosophy and failed project, a project failed for ever, or should its present state be treated as a passing phase, or a transitional stage in "A Long Revolution". Much is at stake on our response to this vital question, specially in a country like India.

6
On Return to Marxism as a Scientific Enterprise

Marxism is a whole human science.

—D.P. Mukerji
"Lament for Economics: Old and New"
The Economic Weekly, November 14, 1959

What we need, therefore, is some kind of a dual recognition of the role and reach of class that take into account its non-uniqueness as well as its transformational functions...

Class is neither the only concern, nor an adequate proxy for other forms of inequality, and yet we do need class analysis to see the ivorking and reach of other forms of inequality and differentiation. Class is not quite like any other source of inequality; it has ubiquitous relevance. The broadening of our understanding of diverse sources of deprivation over the last few decades has certainly been a positive development, and yet class remains as important as ever and the focus on it cannot be relaxed except at a heavy loss.

—Amartya Sen
Class in India, 33rd Jawaharlal Nehru Memorial Lecture
New Delhi, November 13, 2001

There are few countries in the world where the gap between the actual and the potential is as vast as it is in India, although there are also few countries where closing that gap appears as difficult as it does in India.... "Whether the Indian people's tortuous road will have to go through a phase of facism or whether they will be spared that ordeal, only history can show.

—Paul Baran
The Political Economy of Growth, India 1958: pp. xiv; 251

I

The present collection of essays and articles is a revised and enlarged edition of the book first published in 1986 under the title *Marxism and Social Revolution in India and Other Essays*. Twenty-two essays and articles, sixteen from the old collection and six fresh additions, have been put together in this new collection. Even though they were written for different times and different occasions during the last two decades and a half, they have a unifying thread connecting them with each other. The title of the book partly gives expression to what connects them to each other in a basic way. The essays are not just of historical interest. They raise issues having contemporary relevance as explained in this Introduction.

The essays are mainly addressed to non-professionals from the wider intelligentsia and not just to the professional experts and specialists. The aim of these writings is in an important measure to promote a dialogue between activists having a keen interest in the fruits of scientific enquiry and scholars having the desire to share the experiences of those who are grappling with socio-economic problems at the practical level. One must also take note of the fact that some of the leading activists were and are outstanding scholars in their own right and some of the scholars have been involved in activism of one kind or another, specially in fieldwork at the ground level. And yet conceptually the scholars and activists belong to two different categories and the problem of dialogue and interaction between them has become far more complex and more difficult over the years. Understanding and appreciating each other's point of view has also become more complex and difficult in recent years on account of absence of forums for a dialogue and of communication modes.

It may be noted that in the pre-independence period activists and scholars were more genuinely involved in an intimate interaction and dialogue and both had gained enormously from such interaction and dialogue and felt enriched by it. In the post-independence era such interaction and dialogue has unfortunately become less and less and perhaps non-existent. This is a great loss to both scholars and activists.

In the post-independence era social science has grown enormously in diverse fields and social scientists have much to offer to social and political activists. But the problem of communicating the fruits of social enquiry to social and political activists has become as difficult as the need for it is quite urgent. Radical activists often appear to work with ideas and perceptions which have become obsolete with the passage of time or have been shown to be obsolete by advanced social enquiry. And this is true as much of Marxist activists as of activists of other persuasions.

And yet it is as important for activists to be knowledge-responsive (and not knowledge-proof as the late economist, Raj Krishna, had lamented) as it is for scholars to be problem-sensitive and socially concerned. This is the central concern underlying the present exercise.

The present volume has been divided into five sections. Section 1 carries the key essay of the volume and three other articles grouped under the title "Marxism in India: Renewal or Regression". Section II has seven essays and articles grouped under "India in Transition: Ideology and Class Formation". Section III has ten pieces grouped under "Labouring Poor: Victims of the System or Agents of Revolution". Section IV carries the "Epilogue" embodying reflections on the question whether the socialist project has lost its relevance for our times or whether its failure is a phase in a Long Revolution. Section V comprises Appendices under the title "Marxism and the Indian Marxists: Views and Counter-Views". Reproduced in this section are reviews and comments on the first edition of the book by two leading Marxist intellectuals combining theory with practice. The others are eminent Marxist analysts of the Indian situation with different professional backgrounds. But despite their different backgrounds, all of them share a common vision and a lifelong commitment to Marxism and Social Revolution in India. This volume is greatly enriched by their contributions.

These critical responses to my own reflections and observations throw up many basic issues which require deeper study and further reflections from academic scholars as well as social and political activists. I hope that persons more competent and experienced than me and having greater intellectual capabilities and practical experiences will carry forward this ongoing discourse so that it generates more light in the years to come. One of the basic premises of the volume is that the social and political praxis in India is far richer than the radical theoretical responses that it has generated. In fact, one of the younger leaders of the CPM has recently acknow-ledged "the neglect of theory by the Indian Marxist movement" and "inadequate resources provided for theoretical work." (Prakash Karat 2001: 12-13)

I strongly feel that the vast intellectual potential of Indian Marxism has remained largely untapped because of the defacto censorship—the formidable formal and informal constraints—that had been imposed by organised Marxism on free enquiry, free dialogue and discussion. This was in total defiance of Marx's own credo formulated by him at the very start of his active intellectual life: "Criticism, relentless criticism, relentless in the sense that it will shrink neither from its own conclusions nor from conflict with the powers-that-be!"

It must be noted that the pursuit of scientific enquiry recognises no extra-scientific authority outside its own sphere. Why Marxism had its intellectual flowering when in opposition and why it had its worst period of decline and stagnation when it became the ruling doctrine and a prisoner of dogmatism and orthodoxy buttressed by the force of political authority are issues which the Marxists have ignored with disastrous consequences. It is still an unresolved question how to reconcile the need of the political enterprise for authority with the imperatives of scientific enterprise for freedom from authority!

From this wider perspective it is obvious that the crisis of Indian Marxism cannot be fully resolved without a conscious break with the past and without a courageous attempt to *return to Marxism as a serious scientific enterprise.* And the time is ripe for it. Marxism without the support of state power and Marxism liberated from its identification with the state apparatus or the Establishment as its legitimising ideology confronts an era of new opportunities for its creative renewal and rejuvenation.

Marxists, however, can return to Marxism as a scientific enterprise only if they are willing to reverse and restate Marx's famous dictum: "Revolutionaries have so far tried to change the world. The need is there to first understand it." If this new dictum is accepted, vast treasures of new knowledge contributed in diverse fields by modern scientific enterprise will be available to Marxists for moving towards a new intellectual synthesis more relevant for our time and having more solid and sound empirical basis.

We must not forget that modern scientific enterprise neither began nor ended with Marx. If Marx built on the foundations provided by his predecessors, his contemporaries and successors also benefited from him and sometimes transcended him. It was a fatal tendency on the part of important sections of the Marxists in the post-Marxian era to begin treating Marxism itself as the whole of modern knowledge and to create insurmountable barriers between the Marxists and the non-Marxists and between the Marxist and non-Marxist streams of knowledge. Both the Marxists and the non-Marxists were vastly impoverished by a formidable China Wall separating the Marxist and non-Marxist practitioners of social science during the era of the Cold War and even after the end of the era of the Cold War.

Perhaps Marxism as a scientific enterprise had a dramatic re-entry in the Western centres of learning with the end of the Cold War than in the institutions wedded to Marxism. Marx's questions, Marxist concepts and categories and methods of thinking and enquiry have been internalised by modern social science to a much greater extent than Marxists have internalised non-Marxian contributions to knowledge. And this restoration of contact with Marxism as a scientific enterprise in social science centres has opened new ways of illumination of changing social reality and the changing human condition of our times.

A few illustrations will indicate the newly emerging intellectual scenario that I have in mind. The new possibilities of illumination created by the interaction between Marxian and non-Marxian approaches also show how the charge that "the major theoretical advances today take their point of departure from outside the mode of production", the classical Marxist category, does not take note of emerging possibilities and trends in social science enquiry. (Sham Lal 2001: 78) Similarly, the judgement that "not one of the five or six current versions of Marxism can cope with the complexities of the technological and other changes that are transforming life in different ways all over the world" is based on a frozen view of yesterday's trends in Marxism and not on the dynamic view of tomorrow's trends.

The fact of the matter is that the new lines of advance of knowledge are emerging not by "taking their point of departure from outside the mode of production" (that is, the *class* structure factor) but by exploring the role and dynamics of the *other factors* in conjunction with the class factor. If a totally mode-of-production-centred (or class-centred) explanation has proved extremely counterproductive, flawed, partial and inadequate, an explanatory framework which totally excludes the class factor in the analysis of issues of gender, caste, religion, ethnicity, communication, ecology (which are the post-modern preoccupations) is also extremely inadequate, partial, flawed and even counter-productive.

II

True insight into the influences of the *class* factor emerges when seen in conjunction with *other factors* and *vice versa*. In isolation from the *class* factor the insight into the role of *other factors* is neither fully meaningful and adequate in theoretical terms nor in operational terms. And the same is true of the other non-class factors. The *class* and *non-class* factors have to be explored in conjunction with each other for understanding the complex social reality. For this new perspective on the Marxian category of *class* in conjuction with *non-class* factors we are indebted to the contribution of a leading social scientist of our times, Amartya Sen, who is not a Marxist by commitment but has done much more than many Marxists put together for trying to incorporate the basic Marxian insights into the mainstream of social science enquiry. Highly illuminating from this point of view is Amartya Sen's 33rd Jawaharlal Nehru Memorial Lecture *Class in India* delivered on November 13, 2001 at New Delhi. To quote Amartya Sen:

> Class is not only important on its own, it can also magnify the impact of other contributors to inequality, enlarging the penalties imposed by them. The integration of class in a consolidated understanding of injustice is of paramount importance given the need to address simultaneously different sources of inequality, related to class, gender, community, caste, etc. and the overwhelming relevance of class in the working of the other contributions to inequality.
> (Amartya Sen 2001:3)

Amartya Sen's observations quoted above which unfold a wholly new kind of research agenda also open up new possibilities of illumination of social existential reality by employing creative and interactional, multi-dimensional and multi-directional, modes of class analysis rather than a mechanistic, unidimensional and unidirectional model. The insights from such new explanations are bound to be not only far more light-bearing but also infinitely more fruit-bearing in the sense of their much greater efficacy and fruitfulness for action and interventions by societal agencies.

How social science has gained from the impact of Marxism or from incorporating Marxian insights can also be seen from the writings of M.N. Srinivas, a leading sociologist who is at the ideological level very remote from having any sympathy with Marxism and who in fact is known for his liberal-cum-conservative social orientation and outlook. And yet in his seminal essay on "Development of Sociology and Social Anthropology in India" (1973), written jointly with M.N. Panini, Srinivas is prompted to take note of "the influence of Marxism in Indian sociology" and to state that

> the Marxist star is rising in Indian sociology both due to the inherent strength and appeal of the Marxist approach and to the popularity of the writings of thinkers such as C. Wright Mills, Herbert Marcuse, Andre Gunder Frank and others.

In Srinivas' view,

> the recent radicalisation of the Indian political scene is also a factor contributing to the popularity of Marxist writings.
>
> (M.N. Srinivas 1973: 180)

It is obvious that though most Indian Marxists were clinging to their deep prejudices against Srinivas and had deep reservations about his kind of sociology, Srinivas in the true liberal scholarly tradition was able to shake off some of his prejudices against Marxism and the Marxists to take note of the positive side of their contribution to the study of Indian society and even to internalise some of the positive features of the Marxian way of exploring and understanding social reality. How Marxism had made a powerful impact on the thinking process of Srinivas in his study of the Indian problems is exemplified by his highly thought-provoking and illuminating essay under the title "On Living in a Revolution". The essay is path-breaking not only because of his intellectual daring to opt for the concept of "revolution" for the exploration of social change in post-independence India not just as a rhetoric but as an analytical category. Central to this explanation in terms of the category of "revolution" is the focussing on "conflicts"—conflicts connected specially to the inequalities relating to "class", "caste" and "gender" as the motive force of this revolution". The recognition of the positive role of conflicts in promoting this "revolution" is a qualitative advance from Srinivas' previous interpretations of Indian society in terms of structural continuity, or in terms of traditional institutions and values playing what he calls a "cohesive role".

This is not the place to undertake a full evaluation of M.N. Srinivas' sociology from a Marxian perspective but to indicate how social scientists in different fields have been enriched and benefited by an encounter with Marxism. But the Marxists themselves have by and large abstained from a similar encounter with non-Marxian interpretations of Indian social reality offered by sociologists like Srinivas.

Before I pursue this point further, I must mention that the older generation of Marxists had sometimes shown a willingness to know and benefit from the contributions of non-Marxian social scientists. I recall how E.M.S. Namboodiripad had expressed curiosity during the early 1960s about the studies by sociologists on Indian society specially on caste and when he was put in touch with the work of M.N. Srinivas, he had expressed a desire to meet Srinivas. A meeting was arranged between the two which proved very fruitful and E.M.S. Namboodiripad's book. *The Economics and Politics of the Socialist Pattern* draws very richly from the insights and findings contributed by M.N. Srinivas on caste and the village. This encounter with E.M.S. even softened Srinivas who admitted that he had to rethink some of his views on Indian Marxists after his meeting with E.M.S. Namboodiripad whom he described as an outstanding intellectual, apart from being an outstanding political leader of national stature. Namboodiripad had also made a more general self-critical observation in his book mentioned above which is worth reproducing. Namboodiripad had remarked:

> I should also mention here that a feeling has of late grown within me that those of us who have been engaged in heated debates on the problems connected with the socialist pattern have been doing so without digesting the material collected and conclusions drawn by a host of scholars and research workers in the field of social

> science. Our failure in this respect is, I believe, one of the major reasons why we are unable to make a proper evaluation of the actual developments taking place in the country and on its basis to unify the patriotic, democratic and socialist forces in the country.
>
> (E.M.S. Namboodiripad 1966: VIII)

This was a self-critical statement by an outstanding Indian Marxist which has not lost its relevance even today. Indian Marxists need to review their past praxis in the light of this broad guideline provided by Namboodiripad.

Srinivas' theme of 'On Living in a Revolution' or, in other words, the inner dynamics of the "revolution" in India in theoretical as well as empirical terms offers a fruitful area of scientific exploration from both Marxian and non-Marxian perspectives. The question is: What theoretical revision and reformulation does the classical Marxist view of "revolution" as "revolution of small conscious minorities at the head of unconscious masses" (Engels, *War of the Classes*, 1895) require in the context of revolutionary possibilities created by political democracy interpreted in its broadest and not in its limited sense? This is a scientific project which has to be seriously pursued specially in the light of the Indian experience. Srinivas' theme "On Living in a Revolution" thus has wide-ranging implications with reference to India. It must also be stressed that Indian Marxists have been inclined towards stressing the limitations and inadequacies of political democracy from the point of view of the emancipation of the oppressed classes than its radical possibilities and potentialities.

Indian Marxists are showing the same negative attitude in their overestimation of the constraints of Indian democracy as they had shown earlier in their overemphasis on the constraints of Indian nationalism and its leaders during the era of the freedom struggle.

It must be noted that Marxists have been accustomed to form judgements on this issue more on the basis of the classical Marxist position which was conditioned by the circumstances of Marx's times. Thus, the Indian Marxist view was based largely on a priori reasoning than on the basis of hard empirical examination. Such an approach is, however, totally alien to Marx's own approach which was committed to serious empirical investigation.

Gunnar Myrdal's remarks on this question are highly penetrating and pertinent:

> I also feel inclined to express that Marx, behind all his interest in constructing abstract models of the 'laws of movement of capitalist society' was fundamentally an empiricist. He was, therefore, against using anyone as an authority for conclusions about the shape of reality. At least twice in his writings he expressed scorn for 'Marxists' of his time. It seems likely that a hundred years later he would have been sterner in his condemnation of the exegetes. If Marx were living today he would know and take into account all that we now know but that he could not have known a century or more ago.
>
> (Gunnar Myrdal 1970: 459)

III

From the above it is obvious that the theoretical legacy which the present-day Indian Marxists have inherited from Marx and from the post-Marx generations of Marxists including the Indian Marxist has to be critically reappraised in the light of recent advances in the diverse fields of knowledge and also in the light of positive and negative praxological interventions by all those who have been consciously trying to transform society in India and elsewhere. The questions relevant in today's context are in many fundamental respects different from those which Marx or his successors had set before themselves. To try to grapple with today's and tomorrow's questions on the basis of yesterday's theory or on the basis of yesterday's answers to these questions would produce disastrous consequences. In fact, it has already produced disastrous consequences.

The cataclysmic shift to the extreme Right in Indian national politics and tremendous strength acquired by forces of religious fundamentalism and political reaction are not accidental happenings. The serious errors of omission and commission and the flawed perceptions and flawed practice by all those who constituted the main forces of the Indian revolution have contributed in no insignificant measure to the aggravation of this internal crisis of Indian nationalism. The Marxists of all persuasions and hues have also seriously contributed through their dogmatism on the one hand and opportunism on the other towards creating and accentuating this crisis.

"On Living in a Revolution" as defined by Srinivas seems to have turned into its very opposite, that is, into "On Breaking Away from a Revolution" if not yet into "On Living in a Counter-Revolution".

A crisis situation also offers opportunity for self-introspection, self-correction and self-renewal. This is also true of Indian Marxism. Indian Marxism was the child of the Indian Enlightenment and also one of its vital promoters. With its deep roots in the Indian Enlightenment, it has a great potential for leading India from the darkness of unreason into the light of reason.

The unfinished Indian revolution cannot go forward today without holding in its hands the torch of reason and the banner of Charaiveti Charaiveti (March Forward, March Forward)! At the present moment when Indian tradition is falsely invoked to thwart and derail the forward march of the Indian people, revolutionaries must learn to tap the resources of hope and light from within the radical Indian tradition. They must give a new meaning to the age-old concepts of *Moksha* and of *Tamso Ma Jyotirgamaya* (Lead me from darkness to light)! These conceptions must be freed from their other-worldly and individualistic (that is, traditionalistic) interpretations and given a this-worldly, people-oriented and forward-looking connotation relevant to our times. In their new meanings they can become powerful resources of the people in their march from ignorance to enlightenment and from resignation to resistance.

Indian Marxism, in other words, must go native in order to be truly relevant and creative in the present context. This means a painful transition from Eurocentric Marxism to India-oriented (or East-oriented) Marxism. This means that Marxism has to first struggle against its own ignorance of radical Indian tradition and its own alienation from the native milieu including the native idiom. Then alone Marxism can come to its own in India. Then alone it can help to bring closer as co-fighters the radical intelligentsia that thinks and the labouring masses that work and suffer. This was the dream of young Marx for which he laboured, suffered and struggled all his life.

According to Marx, radical theory finds in the labouring poor its material weapon while the labouring poor find in radical theory its intellectual weapon. This Marxian premise of revolution is as valid today as it was then when it was made.

Notes and References

1. Sham Lal, "History Rebuffs Marxism", *A Hundred Encounters*, Rupa & Co., New Delhi, 2001.
2. M.N. Srinivas, "On Living in a Revolution and Other Essays", Oxford University Press, New Delhi, 1992.
3. E.M.S. Namboodiripad, *The Economics and Politics of the Socialist Pattern*, People's Publishing House, New Delhi, 1966.
4. Gunnar Myrdal, *Marxism: The Challenge of World Poverty*, Penguin Books, 1971.

7

Some Fundamental Aspects of Socialist Transformation in India*

The fundamental aspects of socialist transformation in India need to be discussed with reference to the Indian experience as well as to the international experience. This article provides a basis for discussion and rethinking and is not a statement of fixed views, understanding and beliefs on this question. Considering the fact that socialist action in India has not always followed adequate theoretical and philosophical preparation, it is pertinent to reverse Marx's statement and reformulate it as: "Socialists have so far tried to change the world. The need is there to understand it while trying to change it."

In recent years the attention of the political elite, the intelligentsia and the people in India has been focussed on the immediate problems to the point of overlooking long-term problems and perspectives. But to attempt to find solutions to the economic and social problems of the country in isolation from the long-term interests and perspectives is as undesirable as it is counter-productive.

It must also be recalled that under Jawaharlal Nehru's leadership, socialism, secularism, and democracy were accepted as the basis of a unifying world-view. Socialism was accepted as the key concept serving as the directing principle of economic and social planning. We would plead for a return to this principle not only as a directive but also as the operating principle of

* Prepared in collaboration with the late Prof. V.K.R.V. Rao, eminent social scientist and builder of social science institutions in India.

Indian economic and social planning. We also indicate the socio-political conditions under which socialism can be transformed into such an operating principle.

Before taking up the question of socialist transformation, we shall try to define the concept of a socialist society. What are the basic elements of a socialist society which make it different from other types of societies? We are distinguishing between a society making a transition to socialism on the one hand and a mature socialist society on the other. That is to say, we are distinguishing transitional economic patterns on the road to the socialist goal on the one hand and a mature socialist pattern on the other. Without a clear conception of what the socialist society as an ideal type is it is not possible to steer the process of transition in the socialist direction. All patterns of transition involve compromises. But whether the compromise facilitates transition towards the goal or involves the sacrifice of the goal can be decided only if the goal is always kept in view. The vast tension and turmoil which prevails in socialist countries stems, in our view, from the fact that obsolete transitional patterns have a tendency to get solidified and to turn, after a point, into impediments to the realisation of the socialist ideal. The tension between the immediate and the fundamental, the specific and the universal should, therefore, be creatively resolved at every turning point when the free expression of the people's creative energy and the productive forces is stultified due to the rigidity of the transitional institutional arrangements.

Ideal Socialist Society

In our view a society is socialist only if it satisfies the following basic conditions. We have only selected the basic and ignored the subsidiary attributes of socialism. We have further selected the universal attributes and ignored the question of the specific national form in which universal attributes find expression.

1. The economic system is based not on the private ownership of the basic means of production and private appropriation of the surpluses but on the social ownership of the basic means

of production and the social appropriation of the surpluses. By ruling out the dominance of the principle of private property in basic means of production, and therefore by ruling out the directive role of private profit, the socialist system eliminates the economic basis of exploitation of the producing masses by a narrow propertied class. By affirming the social character of appropriation and not merely social ownership of the means of production it also guards against the emergence of new forms of economic exploitation whereby the public sector or the bureaucracy covertly or overtly appropriates the fruits of labour of the workers, both mental and manual.

2. Socialism is associated with the total commitment to the scientific approach. It puts a high premium on the continuous exploration of scientific knowledge and technology and their application to all spheres of production in a planned manner so as to ensure an uninterrupted growth of the productive forces of the national and international communities. Condition (1) ensures that this economic growth is not used for the benefit of a narrow class but that it is used for the benefit of the entire community.
3. Socialism is committed to the closing of the vast gulf created by capitalism between manual and mental workers, villages and towns, and between the developed countries and under-developed countries. It is also committed to the abolition of economic and social discrimination on the basis of sex, race, colour and nationality.
4. Socialism involves the release of the creative energy and initiative of the people on a vast scale and this is not possible without raising the cultural level of the people. Socialism, therefore, implies a new cultural ethos, a new social ethics, a new educational system and new motivations. Without such a re-education of the people on a vast scale, socialism has all the possibilities of degenerating into "bureaucratic"

socialism and leading to the suppression of individuality and political freedom.

5. Socialism insofar as it is based on the development of science and technology and on the positive participation of the people in managing social affairs should subsume full democracy—the rule of the people, by the people and for the people. Democracy without socialism is incomplete in so far as men must be equal in the economic sphere before they can be really equal in the political sphere. Socialism is also incomplete without democracy to the extent that without freedom of thought, the right of dissent and popular participation in decision-making and their implementation, the potentialities created by socialism for the flowering of the human personality and for the full release of creative energy of the people would remain unrealised.

   One must also distinguish between a socialist democracy on the one hand and capitalist democracy on the other. As envisaged by Marx, democracy finds its fullest extension in a society where class exploitation and dominance are eliminated. Similarly, socialism finds its fulfilment, both at the level of ends and means, in democracy which abolishes the concept of natural superiority of the elite over the masses. In a capitalist democracy there is inadequate scope for the working masses to share in economic power and for self-management in the economic sphere. Socialist democracy should, ideally speaking, provide full scope for the common people to become capable for self-management both in the political and economic spheres.

6. Finally, socialism, specially in countries which are late comers into the arena of modern economic growth, is not to be regarded only as a means of achieving rapid transition to a modern economy under conditions of massive economic backwardness. The superiority of socialism to capitalism lies not just in being an instrument for achieving a higher rate of economic growth within a short span of

> time. The superiority of socialism has to be demonstrated in terms of its contribution as much to the quality of life, which is non-measurable, as to the strengthening of the material base of social existence, which is measurable in quantitative terms. From this standpoint one must reckon with not only the human costs of economic stagnation and underdevelopment but also those of economic development untempered by cultural values and norms of cooperation, sharing and human solidarity.

In countries with vast rural communities such a commitment to human values and norms involves the carrying forward of as much of the rich legacies and traditions of the past civilisation of each country as it involves the creation of new forms of civilisation suited to the modern period. In other words, socialism is not the blind destruction of the past, it must demarcate itself from the destructive role of capitalism in regard to the values and norms which were worthy of preservation but were eliminated by the logic of capitalist development.

What we have presented above is an *ideal type* of socialist society rather than the picture of any particular society in any particular country. The construction of an ideal type is necessary for it helps one to assess in what respects any particular society approximates to or diverges from the socialist ideal. This procedure is specially necessary for the assessment of transitional systems as the transitional phase does not always permit the simultaneous pursuit of a multiplicity of objectives. During transition one objective may be in conflict with another.

Having defined a socialist society we now deal with the problems of transition to a socialist society. We must remember that in the West the idea of socialism was the fruit of an Industrial Revolution. The industrialisation of the economy and the achievement of a socialist society were envisaged in classical socialist thought as two separate and distinct phases. In Western countries capitalism had already solved the problem of capital accumulation. Socialism was expected to bring about a more rational utilisation of the productive capacity created by capitalism in the interest of the entire community and to solve the problem of human alienation.

This classical view, however, is not valid for the underdeveloped countries of the contemporary world which suffer less "from the contradictions of capitalist development and much more from the contradictions arising from the incompleteness of capitalist development" (Lenin). As latecomers the underdeveloped countries have to make a decisive break from poverty and underdevelopment in a few decades which the Western countries achieved in a few centuries. They have no option but to achieve simultaneously both industrial development and social emancipation (i.e. emancipation from inequality and injustice).

India's Case Different

There are many who believe that countries like India should first achieve an industrial revolution before thinking of a socialist transformation. What, in effect, these people suggest is that the country should first have a long period of capitalist development before it can hope to think of a socialist transformation.

Those holding this view seem to have no sense of history and no consciousness of the compulsions of the new epoch in which we are living. In countries such as India the whole sequence of social evolution with which we are familiar from Western history has been reversed. In the West parliamentary democracy and a welfare state followed the maturing of an industrial revolution. In India the framework of parliamentary democracy and of a welfare state have preceded an industrial revolution. History moves forwards rather than backwards. In this vastly changed social background we can no more conceive of a long period of intensified exploitation of the masses for capitalist development; nor can we conceive of prolonged political subjugation of the masses under capitalist hegemony as in the West. Neither an unrestricted capitalist growth in the economic sphere nor an exclusive capitalist hegemony in the political sphere are possible in the present period. Under the new socio-political conditions the only long-term economic perspective is that of the progressive subordination of private capital to social purpose and the progressive increase in the weight of social capital in the economic structure. Similarly, the only satisfactory political perspective is that of the increasing weight of the non-capitalist classes in general and the working masses in particular in the country's state structure.

This means that in the new historical context the forces of industrial revolution or economic development should be so channelised that instead of promoting the hegemony of private capital in the economy they should serve to promote the predominance of social capital. Socialist transformation also means that the economy is pulled out of the state of stagnation and is firmly set on the path of modern economic growth and development. In other words, economic development should reinforce the trend towards socialist transformation, and socialist transformation should reinforce the processes of economic development.

Classical Strategy

In considering the problem of the strategy of socialist transformation reference to the classical socialist strategy is very necessary.

The strategy of socialist transformation adopted and practised by the Soviet Union can be called the classical socialist strategy. Here a workers' party captured political power with the support of workers and peasants through an armed overthrow of the Czarist regime and thereafter established a new regime called the dictatorship of the proletariat. This regime had to face fierce political and armed opposition from a civil war and from aggression by capitalist states. It was forced, therefore, not strictly by economic but more urgently by political considerations to expropriate private capital and liquidate the capitalist sector first in banking, trade, industry, transport, etc. and later also in agriculture. What is important to note is that this process of total socialisation of the national economy had to be accelerated not entirely in response to the strategy laid down earlier but on account of unforeseen political compulsions. As Lange points out :

> All that Lenin wrote about State capitalist forms of development, regarding the integration of the capitalist sector with the socialist economy establishing a peaceful process of socialist construction, was exploded by the civil war. (Oscar Lange, *Problems of Political Economy of Socialism*, PPH, Delhi, 1959, p. 46).

The expropriation of private capital was put on the agenda due to the need to destroy the economic base of political reaction, or of landlord-capitalist opposition, which was conspiring to subvert the workers' regime.

The other important feature of the classical socialist strategy was that socialist transformation served along with economic and social planning as a conscious means of forced capital accumulation and industrialisation. The classical socialist strategy is, therefore, significant not merely as a method of eliminating private capitalism and accomplishing socialist transformation. Its significance lies in serving as an alternative road to modern economic development. The appeal of this strategy for backward countries lies in its contribution to transforming a backward economy into an industrially developed one within a few decades.

The socialist pattern demonstrated its superiority over the capitalist pattern by serving as an effective means for the mopping up of surpluses from all branches of the economy; of imposing effective restraint on consumption; of efficient distribution of scarce wage goods and services during a period characterised by concentration of investment in the capital goods sector; of mobilising the entire society for hard work, austerity and sacrifice on a vast scale.

In considering a strategy of socialist transformation for India we should distinguish between the general significance of the Soviet model and its unique features determined by the peculiar circumstances of that country and the international situation of that period. The Soviet experience involved a strategy that emerged in response to the challenge of building up socialism in one country in the context of the resistance from the capitalist and landlord classes inside and the capitalist encirclement from outside. Further, the absence of democratic traditions in the country and the hostility of capitalist powers to the Soviet regime conspired to convert this strategy into one of socialist transformation without democratic institutions and with the large-scale use of the coercive apparatus of the state. Again, these very circumstances not only forced a postponement of democracy, also made "tightening of the belt" a necessary part of the economic strategy for a long time. The Soviet Union, therefore, was able to convert socialist transformation into a means of economic development. But it had to postpone the achievement of some basic ingredients of political democracy and mass welfare to the next historical stage.

No Imitation of Soviet Model

In the above background, the tendency to universalise the Soviet model should be avoided in large overpopulated countries in taking decisions about the policies to be pursued towards the capitalist sector; in discussing the compatibility of socialist transformation with democracy in the transitional phase; in determining the allocations between heavy industry and consumer goods; and specially in evolving socialist forms for agriculture, in a situation of predominance of small producers deriving their livelihood from land and having no prospect of absorption outside agriculture in the foreseeable future. Mechanical imitation of the Soviet model has had harmful consequences in many countries. At the same time the general or transferable lessons of the Soviet model that can be treated as valid for socialist transformation elsewhere should also be fully taken into account. Here the lesson emerging from the Soviet experience pertains to the relation that should prevail between economic planning for socialist transformation and private concentration of economic power. Oscar Lange who was requested to sum up the relevance of the Soviet and East European models on this question wrote as follows:

> It can be stated as a general principle that successful planning for economic development must imply the abolition—or at least neutralisation—of such concentration of economic power as would block the realisation of the plan. What this involves in terms of concrete measures will vary with particular historical circumstances of each country and may even vary at different stages of a country's planning experience. The concrete solution will depend on how such private concentrations of economic power align themselves with the general objectives of national economic planning. Their alignment, in turn, may depend on the extent to which the government charged with the task of realisation of a national plan of economic development is able to marshal the support of the broadest sections of the people and of their organisations. Beyond this no general statement can be made. The particular application to a country like India must be undertaken by persons more competent than the writer of these lines. (Oscar Lange, *Essays on Economic Planning*, ISI, Calcutta, 1960).

It must be remembered in the above context, that the strategy of socialist transformation required an anti-capitalist direction right from the start in the Soviet Union, assuming the form of nationalisation of banking, industry and trade and of a ruthless drive towards collectivisation of agriculture. Further, in the Soviet Union, a temporary retreat from anti-capitalist measures had to be resorted to under NEP. In ex-colonial and semi-feudal countries like India, capitalism had a politically revolutionary role in the anti-colonial struggle and has vast possibilities of playing a positive role in continuing the war of independence on the economic plane. The socialist strategy in India may thus have to accommodate a capitalist sector and its growth for a long period of time as part of the prolonged transition towards socialism.

Nehru's Mixed Economy

In considering the strategy for a socialist transformation in India we cannot thus start with a clean slate. India under the leadership of Jawaharlal Nehru had evolved its own strategy of socialist transformation. The key concept of this strategy has been the concept of a *mixed economy* (within the framework of a parliamentary democracy), as the transitional form for India's socialist transformation. This concept implied the rejection of the idea of immediate socialisation of the economy because of the need for mobilising all productive classes, including the capitalist elements, for national economic development.

Nehru's conception of a mixed economy thus implied a regulated private sector and a fast-expanding public sector in basic and strategic industries and in power, transport, etc., and a cooperative sector in agriculture, with the overall direction of development by the state through its control of the commanding heights of the economy (like banking, credit, trade, etc). This was presented by Nehru as the strategy for ushering in a society industrially developed on the one hand and socialistic on the other. It was also presented as a non-classical or a middle-path strategy of economic and social development. It is now widely recognised that this middle-path has given India an independent economic base and ensured a sharp break from the economic stagnation and underdevelopment associated with the colonial period. At the same time, it is also recognised that formidable obstacles have come in the way of further progress towards socialist transformation or economic development. Consensus, however, does not exist on the causes of this economic stalemate or setback. Did the failure lie in the very conception of a 'mixed economy' or in implementing the basic principles and procedures laid down for operating a mixed economy? Is it necessary now to abandon the concept of a mixed economy to remove the obstruction in the path of socialist transformation? These questions are now being debated in the country.

A basic weakness of the present debate is that it is being conducted without reference to concrete realities and experiences. The ideologues of the private sector press for abandoning the concept of the mixed economy in favour of greater freedom to the private sector. The ideologues of the Left also press for abandoning the concept of the mixed economy but in favour of greater regimentation in the economy and the extension of state ownership and control to the sector under private ownership and control. In particular, they demand an attack on "big business monopolies" which in their view have registered a phenomenal growth since independence, and have now emerged as colossal concentrations of economic power, opposing planned development and socialist transformation.

Realities of the Indian Situation

These questions can be resolved only by taking note of the realities of the present Indian situation. There has not been enough investigation, however, of these realities. The ideologues of the Right talk as if the forces of a virile capitalism are being thwarted by injudicious and thoughtless state interference. The ideologues of the Left, on the other hand, seem to suggest that what is lacking in the Indian situation is the institutional framework of a full-fledged socialist economy, and that if the latter is introduced the economy would forge ahead with a new momentum.

Neither of the two assessments constitutes an approximation to the realities of the Indian situation. The ideologues of the Right have to note that capitalism in a country of subcontinental dimensions like India has had an uneven development. In many backward regions of the country Indian capitalism is yet more mercantile, usurious and speculative than industrial. It still carries the dead weight of a feudal, mercantile and colonial past. Does not the history of industrial revolutions confirm the transition from mercantile to industrial forms of capitalism as the most formidable aspect of the transition from the pre-industrial to the industrial economy? Indian experience also confirms this assessment.

Further, we must distinguish between genuine industrialisation which serves to build the basic productive capacity of the economy and is a means of eradicating mass poverty on the one hand and pseudo-industrialisation which serves the consumption needs of the elite on the other. Experience has shown that Indian capitalism has been more prone to the latter than the former. In other words, to allow private capital to operate without judicious state interference does not amount to the release of productive forces in the priority sectois. It may amount to allowing leakages of public resources into non-priority areas. The stimulus to luxury goods production as an unintended consequence of planning in a mixed economy has raised the question of the limits of a mixed economy. Moreover, private capital taking the form of big business has created a serious threat in the form of political corruption. In particular, the connection between the financing patterns of political parties and the dominance of private moneyed interests has been threatening the very growth of a viable democratic framework in the country.

An adequate appraisal of the above factors compels one to conclude that the choice today does not lie between the extremes of unlimited economic freedom to the private sector on the one hand and of unlimited state intervention on the other. The choice in fact lies between an injudicious, partial and ineffective state intervention and a judicious, strategic and effective intervention by the state and other social agencies. Even within capitalism one has to differentiate between the parasitic and the productive forms of capitalism and to use the latter in the national interest, while relentlessly eliminating the scope for the growth of the former. This is a subtle, complex and challenging task which requires the combining of direct methods of economic intervention with the effective use of indirect methods such as public investment, monetary and fiscal devices, pricing policy, etc.

The Right Mixture

One can says in this background, that there is nothing wrong in a mixed economy so long as it is a mixture of the desirable elements. A mixture of the genuinely socialistic and productive capitalist elements working in priority areas is a mixture of the right type. And we can call only such elements, whether capitalist or socialist, genuine or progressive as contribute to the economic independence of the country and also the elimination of mass poverty. In this light a mixture of the semi-feudal and mercantile-cum-usurious capitalist elements on the one hand and of parasitic and unproductive bureaucratic-capitalist elements on the other is a mixture of the wrong type. It has also to be noted that in the Indian rural economy semi-feudalism and exploitative usurious and trading capital are still quite strong if not dominant, even though in disguised forms in many regions of the country. And the effective liquidation of the scope for the growth of these elements should be regarded as fully compatible with the principles of a mixed economy, and even conducive to genuine industrial-capitalist development. Further, the unbridled growth of a capitalist sector in agriculture can also not be treated as desirable in a labour-surplus economy. The containment though not elimination of this capitalist sector and the strengthening of the peasant sector should be regarded as essential prerequisites of a mixed economy of the right type in countries such as India.

The ideologues of the Left also have their blind spots which do not allow them to make a meaningful contribution to the debate on the economic question. Their major weakness is that they tend to consider questions of socialist transformation without fully taking into account the imperatives of economic development in a backward country. They have seldom given thought to the enormous organisational and educational implications of every step in the direction of socialist transformation, if this step is to lead simultaneously to an increase in productivity, economic efficiency and mass welfare. Mere extension of social ownership or increase in the powers of the state by themselves do not contribute to socialism if they do not result in a better allocation and better utilisation of both human and material resources. Further, even if we introduce the full-fledged economic institutional framework of a socialist economy, this does not ensure the automatic utilisation of this framework for socialist objectives. As the experience of many countries including India shows, this framework has degenerated into a vast bureaucratic-socialist empire, a paradise for the power-loving bureaucrats and technocrats. At the same time, it has also been accompanied by a complete lack of identification of the worker with the public sector enterprise resulting in marked economism and in irresponsible trade-unionism, leading to enormous losses in productivity.

Learning from Past Experience

Lessons should be drawn in this respect from the Indian experience itself. The public sector in India even now directly controls certain strategic points in the economy both relating to the infrastructure and to the production of capital goods, industrial inputs, raw material, etc. The state also has powerful instruments for indirectly influencing the economy, viz. monetary and fiscal policies, taxation, credit, price control and licensing policies. And yet, the sectors directly controlled by the government have not always yielded satisfactory results either in terms of economic efficiency or in terms of mass welfare. The very instruments which were expected to promote the national interest or socialist objectives have been used to promote narrow sectional interests. Past experience thus shows that institutions can serve the purpose of achieving socialist aims only if there exists a high level of social consciousness and organisation among every section of society and specially among the weaker sections who have a major stake in socialism. Only if there exists socialist cadres combining dedication to the socialist cause with organisational ability and technical skill, both of a high order, can socialist institutions lead to socialist transformation. In the absence of these the state may have all the commanding heights of the economy in its hands but these may be used not for promoting socialism but for strengthening private economic or bureaucratic or sectional working class power. The state may have all the laws on its statute books for punishing those obstructing the advance to socialism but it may not be able to use this coercive apparatus and thus function as a "soft" state of the Myrdal variety.

Socialist institutional framework, therefore, is a necessary but certainly not a sufficient condition for socialist transformation. In the Soviet Union, for instance, it is not the economic institutions alone which ensured the success of socialism. One has also to take note of the role played by a leader of the calibre and integrity of Lenin and a party of dedicated cadres like the Communist Party. One must also take note of the enormous capacity for hard work and for social discipline created by them by force of personal example under Lenin and even under an important part of the Stalin regime. These non-institutional factors made a tremendous difference in the quality of the functioning of the economic institutions.

Reappraisal Necessary

To sum up, the Nehru strategy of socialist transformation through a mixed economy and within a framework of parliamentary democracy needs a critical re-appraisal in the light of actual experience It requires a fundamental reformulation if it is to deliver the goods and cope with the new economic challenges facing India in the post-Nehru era. The re-formulation of this economic strategy should, in the present stage, make due allowance for the following aspects:

(i) The continuing resilience of landlordism, exploitative non-institutional credit, and trading capital in the rural economy in many regions need to be effectively curbed to create the pre-conditions for a fresh release of the productive forces in the rural economy.

(ii) The growing importance of a capitalist sector in the agriculture of advanced regions, which have been the centres of the so-called Green Revolution, where a policy package needs to be evolved and implemented for tapping the surplus generated in the capitalist sector for taking the new technology to the peasant sector on the one hand and for promoting balanced agro-industrial growth on the other.

(iii) The need for ensuring greater state control in the sphere of distribution of goods and services as an aid to a non-inflationary pattern of development. This presupposes judicious state intervention over trade in agricultural commodities and industrial raw materials, and also the extension of the public sector to the sphere of the production of wage goods and other essential commodities and services entering mass consumption.

(iv) An expansion of the infrastructure facilities for skill formation and the availability of investible funds are required for stimulating enterprise in backward regions and backward classes on a vast scale. These would accelerate the growth of small and medium entrepreneurs within a cooperative or state-sponsored framework, and thus result in broad-basing the process of economic development.

(v) The concentration of private economic power represented by Big Business needs to be effectively neutralised and curbed in the transitional phase, and eliminated over a longer period. Such concentration has no place in a socialist society. However, in the transitional phase characterised by the entrepreneurial lag and by a shortage of essential commodities, certain compromises may be necessary and may require the utilisation of the productive capacity represented by the private sector, for coping with the problem of these acute shortages. These compromises may also be necessary if the alternative course leads to dependence on foreign sources. But these compromises will be politically acceptable only if they do not lead to an increase in the political influence of Big Business and in its capacity to subvert national priorities.

Further, any wise political leadership, while being forced to compromise under the pressure of immediate problems and while choosing the lesser evil, should at the same time take such economic and political measures as would ensure that the private sector operates within a political and economic frame and not outside it. Strong measures should be undertaken for preventing the diversion of investible resources into commodity speculation, conspicuous consumption, production of luxury goods and to ensuring the flow of capital, even private capital, into the production of essential goods and services, and above all to guarding against large-scale bribing and corruption of politicians and administrators by Big Business. A strong political regime committed to national economic independence and to mass interests alone can implement these policies without causing harm to the socialist cause.

(vi) Economic sanctions and measures against the private sector, however, would be politically acceptable and economically justifiable only if the performance of the public sector and state agencies shows qualitative improvement both in terms of economic efficiency and social welfare.

(vii) The main economic weakness of the Indian pattern of mixed economy as a transitional form can be said to lie in its failure to serve as an effective means of surplus mobilisation and capital accumulation, and its utter failure to instil new motivations in either the entrepreneurial, the professional or the working classes.

Reasons for Deviation

In addition, a clear demarcation of the two alternative patterns of a mixed economy should be made. In pattern I of the mixed economy, the state agencies and the public sector provide external economies to the fast-growing private sector or to private concentrations of economic power. The basic decisions of production, distribution, saving and investment, in this case, are taken either by the private sector directly or in response to the pressures of this sector by state agencies. In pattern II the state has the control of strategic points of the economy which are used as commanding heights for determining the main direction of the development of the economy. The private sector in this pattern is subordinated to the overall demands of national development on socialist lines. The state converts in this way the commanding heights also into lucrative heights, ensuring thereby the acceleration of the tempo of capital formation and resource mobilisation. As between the two patterns of the mixed economy, the Indian pattern during the past twenty-five years has conformed more to the former rather than to the latter.

This was, however, not entirely in conformity with Nehru's strategy of socialist transformation. To understand the reasons for this departure one has to switch over from the plane of the economics of Nehru's strategy to the plane of its political economy. In other words, Nehru and Nehru's successors went wrong not so much in formulating an appropriate economic strategy as in failing to clearly identify and build the human agents of economic transformation. They were only partially successful in creating the *socio-cultural* and *political* conditions for effective implementation of this economic strategy. The failure, thus, was on the part of the Indian political and intellectual elite as a whole in taking a narrowly economic rather than a politico-economic and sociological view of the process of economic development and socialist transformation suited to an ex-colonial and semi-feudal economy. In other words, the fault lay in the failure to formulate the political strategy and to consolidate the social and ethical forces for economic development and socialist transformation. The missing element in the Indian strategy has been political and social mobilisation for economic growth and socialist transformation.

Even those sections of the elite who have a commitment to the socialist ideal have failed to undertake mass education and mobilisation for socialism because of certain basic weaknesses. Partly it is the unwillingness of the new middle class to follow its socialist professions with socialist practice and be ready to share poverty with the less privileged sections of the society. Partly it is the absence on their part to acquire an adequate knowledge and understanding of the Indian social structure and the resistance emanating from it to the socialist cause.

What are the hard points of this structure obstructing socialist transformation and requiring to be neutralised or altered to facilitate the implementation of any economic strategy for socialist transformation? Answers to these questions were sought in the past much less in terms of the Indian experience and realities but more in terms of what was done in other countries. The sharp division and disunity among various sections of the socialist movement in India is also to be attributed partly, if not wholly, to the intellectual lag and to the weakening of the moral fibre. An Indian road to socialism can be evolved as the unifying framework for all sections of the socialist movement only by a better and keener perception of the Indian conditions by the socialist groups. We may recall in this context a meaningful observation of Professor Beni Prasad made in the pre-independence period but which still applies to the period after independence. He observed: "Indian socialism has yet to produce its Karl Marx who is willing to spend, if not twenty years, at least 20 months in the serious study and investigation of an Indian problem."

No Correct Leadership

The other basic weakness has been that the leadership of the socialist movement has come predominantly from upper and intermediate classes and castes and it has remained by and large concentrated in these classes and castes. Even the class composition of the leadership of those calling themselves socialist parties is as upper and middle class based as that of the mixed parties like the Indian National Congress. The Westernised, or more precisely, the Anglicised, and predominantly urban character of the political elite in India has prevented them from active interaction with the Indian masses who are predominantly illiterate and rural in their social character. This gap has led to the continuing lack of education of the masses in the principles of socialism, and their activisation and organisation for the defence and implementation of socialist policies. The widespread laxity and lack of social discipline among all sections of the

Indian society is also partly due to this lack of rapport between the elite and the masses. Similarly, the upper and middle class character of the administrators and the technocrats is also a serious impediment. They are most often apathetic, if not hostile, to socialist objectives. Nothing has been done to restructure or reorient the adminstration to make it favourable to the process of socialist transformation, and yet the implementation of socialist policies has been left entirely to this administration.

Earlier, we identified two alternative economic patterns of a mixed economy, one favourable to capitalist and the other to socialist transformation. We conclude by identifying two alternative political patterns or power structures associated with a mixed economy, within a parliamentary democratic framework. Pattern I is based on a political alliance of the intermediate classes with the upper classes resorting to socialist ideology only to win mass support by using all levers of power to facilitate a type of capitalist development in the interest of a narrow section of the Indian society. Pattern II is based on the political alliance of the have-nots and the intermediate classes using socialist ideology to release mass energy and initiative on a vast scale, and using the levers of power to promote the process of economic development and socialist transformation in a mutually reinforcing manner, in the interest of self-reliance on the one hand and of the widest sections of Indian society, especially of those at the bottom, on the other.

The economic pattern leading to economic growth and socialist transformation is thus inseparable from a political pattern favourable to such growth and transformation. Thus the conclusion is inescapable that the socialist transformation of the Indian economy has been thwarted by powerful obstructions to socialism that exist in the non-economic plane. And it is only by neutralising these non-economic obstructions that success will be achieved in implementing and achieving socialist transformation together with the development of the Indian economy as a fully self-reliant national economy.

8
Imperatives of Renewal of Socialism

The USSR has completed more than seven decades of its existence as the first socialist state of the world. During this period it has been engaged in the epoch-making experiments of creating the framework of a socialist society as a civilisational alternative to Western capitalism. Under Gorbachev's leadership, the Soviet Union has now entered a new and still more adventurous era of self-questioning and self-appraisal in the light of its fundamental socialist vision and principles and its vast and rich experience of building socialism.

The concepts of Glasnost and Perestroika have been thrown up as new concepts of great philosophical and practical significance by this self-questioning process. These concepts also envisage a search for far-reaching socialist rectification and renewal. This search encompasses, in Gorbachev's words, both demolition and reconstruction. Indeed, reconstruction is not possible without demolition. This search thus involves rejecting such obsolete and antiquated institutional patterns and mental orientations as were associated with socialist transition in the formative period. It also involves innovating such new institutional patterns, practices and styles as are suited to the vastly changed conditions and requirements of today. These innovations, far from eroding the socialist framework and relations are bound to strengthen and reinforce the socialist framework and values. With these innovations socialism will begin to free itself from the structural as well as ideological deformations and distortions that originated under the abnormal conditions under which socialist transition occurred after the October Revolution. These distortions also resulted from theoretical inadequacies in comprehending and coping with the complex problems of transition from a predominantly pre-capitalist, pre-democratic and pre-modern stage of Tsarist Russia to the socialist stage.

It is important to remember that inherited theory had envisaged transition from highly developed capitalism to socialism in Western European countries and not transition into *socialism in a single country* as economically, socially, culturally and politically backward as Tsarist Russia. Post-revolutionary Russia was thus called upon to achieve in a single country and in a single leap and under hostile internal and external conditions in a few decades the bourgeois-democratic task, which capitalism had achieved in the West in several centuries, along with the socialist task for which no precedent was provided of history. The roots of structural and ideological deformations of socialism in the USSR lie in this paradox: history set before one of the most backward countries of the world, viz. Tsarist Russia the task of achieving the highest form of social development. The ideal of socialism in the Marxist conception presupposed the prior conditions of Enlightenment and Renaissance, liberty and democracy, and a modern industrial economy based on high levels of capital accumulation, advanced skills and technology and a class conscious proletariat as the predominant class pitched against the concentrated power of the capitalist class. None of these conditions for socialist transition were fulfilled by Russia after the October Socialist Revolution.

The Revolution inherited the worst conditions of medievalism, in terms of widespread illiteracy and socio-cultural backwardness in a mujhik-dominated society, the identification of the bourgeois-landed class with autocracy without any commitment to civil liberties characteristic of a bourgeois polity, an economy dominated by pre-capitalist social relations and primitivism rather than by the capitalist economic formation, an extremely underdeveloped intelligentsia which had yet to experience the emancipating impact of modern enlightenment and renaissance. The grotesque distortions and deformations of socialism in the Soviet Union cannot be understood without taking full cognisance of the historically determined social, economic and political conditions under which the first socialist society had to be formed and to be consolidated. In a nutshell, Russian socialism grew not under ideal conditions of modernity envisaged by Marx but under far from ideal conditions of medievalism inherited by revolutionaries from past history.

In the words of great thinker, philosopher and writer, Romain Rolland, the first socialist society was like the child which had its origins amidst bloody violence; it was a child of a bloody revolution. But from its very birth it was the harbinger of the new age, the age of emancipation of the downtrodden and the disinherited. That is why the birth of the child, i.e. the socialist society, was greeted with joy and hope by forward-looking people all over the world.

The Socialist system had a tremendous appeal for the people of Western industrial capitalist societies as well as to the people of Asian agrarian societies in the first few decades following the Great October Revolution.

The source of its appeal to Western capitalist countries lay in the centrally planned economy, which was the major outcome of the October Socialist Revolution. One should recall how the Western people were stricken by the deep inner crisis of the capitalist economic system as reflected in the Great Depression of the 1930s and in the widespread mass unemployment, immiserisation, insecurity and the destruction of productive protential associated with capitalism before the Second World War. To them the sharp contrast between crisis-ridden capitalism and the planned socialist economy was too obvious to be missed. The Soviet socialist system was then moving with confident strides towards planned development. With its promise of eliminating economic crisis, instability and insecurity and with its assurance for providing fundamental freedoms from want, unemployment, illiteracy, disease, houselessness, socialism appeared to the thinking people of the West in the pre-Second World War world as vastly and qualitatively superior to the Western capitalism rooted in economic anarchy and waste of productive potential. Sidney and Beatrice Webb's book, *Soviet Union: A New Civilisation*, sums up the enlightened Western response to Soviet socialism during that period.

The socialist system of the USSR had a much greater appeal to the people of Asia on the basis of its epoch-making and path-breaking achievement in terms of the socio-economic transformation of one of the most backward regions of the world into an industrially and culturally advanced region competing with the most advanced capitalist country of the world within less than four to five decades. The emergence of the Soviet Union as an industrially developed nation on the basis of a new path of development as an alternative to the capitalist path rendered obsolete Marx's famous statement in the Preface to the first volume of *Capital:* "The industrially developed nation (i.e. England) shows to the industrially backward ones the image of their own future." It is not England "the industrial workshop of the world", which now showed to the Western countries the image of their own future but the Soviet Union which had successfully telescoped the development process extending over several centuries in the past into a few decades. Moreover, in contrast to the Western model which was based on mass exploitation, the Soviet model was based on abolition of conditions of mass exploitation and on concern for mass welfare.

This radiant and appealing picture of Soviet socialism was, however, overshadowed in the post-war world by the discovery of certain dismal and dark features of the socialist pattern of development and the socialist systems in the USSR specially following Khrushchev's revelations of Stalinism.

The bright picture was also overshadowed by certain new dramatic possibilities and challenges which emerged within both the Western capitalist countries as well as the newly-liberated Asian countries like India.

In the Western world there emerged new scientific and technological possibilities which gave a fresh release to the productive forces following the end of the Second World War. Moreover, the emergence of the New Deal and the Keynesian revolution were associated with new concepts of an interventionist state and control of economy and the new techniques of public investment and regulation of market processes which successfully coped with these new strategies and mechanisms in the grave economic crisis. These reset the Western economies on a new path of growth with economic stability. The culmination of these trends was reflected in the German and the Japanese miracles—the rehabilitation of the war-shattered economies of Germany and Japan, and later in the growth miracles of under-developed countries like South Korea and Taiwan.

Further, in many capitalist countries which grew into modem welfare states the anti-poverty programmes and programmes of public education, social security, medical services, housing, etc., led to a new era of growth with social jusuce and national integration. Still further, under people's pressure the concepts of democratic freedoms and of human rights gained a new momentum in Western societies which vastly curbed the oppressive character of the state associated with the early stages of capitalism. These epochal developments in the Western world stood in marked contrast to revelations about the absence of democracy and certain basic human rights (which are associated with free civilised societies) within the Soviet Union. These also stood in marked contrast to the imbalances and distortions as well as slowing down of growth in the USSR. These created a sharp disenchmtanent in the West with the socialist system. The anti-socialist forces exploited this situation to the fullest extent.

A parallel development took place in Asian countries like India which adopted the perspective of growth with social justice within the framework of a parliamentary democracy along with an open society based on international cooperation. The Soviet model of development based on a closed society, a single party rule, absence of democracy and lack of some basic human rights, the marked stagnation in agriculture and in technological progress specially relating to agriculture no longer offered a ready-made model which was worthy of emulation by countries like India. Hence a certain critical attitude to socialism grew among the intelligentsia even in Asian countries like India which, though appreciating the role of planning and selective socialisation of the means of production recognised the necessity of going beyond the Soviet model and of evolving a new model combining democracy and social justice with growth within a framework of non-alignment. In other words, countries like India had to look outside Western capitalism and beyond Soviet socialism, and to learn to combine some of the welfare-promoting redistributive techniques of Western economics with the planning techniques of Soviet socialism.

The epochal significance of Gorbachev's new concepts can be understood fully if we keep the above historical background fully in view. *These new concepts put the Soviet Union once again in the centre of a new dynamism, both moral and intellectual. The Soviet Union emerges as the principal promoter of a dialogue both within and outside the Soviet Union for evolving a new approach and concepts relevant to the new era.* It is from this perspective that we should explore the essence of Glasnost and Perestroika.

Gorbachev's Glasnost and Perestroika seek extension of democracy, rule of law, respect for the individual freedom of conscience and belief for followers of all religions. They reaffirm Marx's original premise of primacy of human values over class values, of pursuing the class struggle in a manner that "it does not lead to the mutual ruin of the contending classes but to a revolutionary, reconstitution of human society" (*Communist*

Manifesto). Gorbachev's concepts reject a hegemonistic approach in favour of pursuing national goals and objectives with overriding concern for the unity of entire mankind and within the framework of a new international order. Gorbachev's world-view encompasses Gandhi's concepts of non-violence as an essential condition for eliminating sources of mutual hatred and animosity which ultimately result in accelerating the arms-race and aggravating the danger of war and which if not checked will in the nuclear age spell the annihilation of entire mankind.

Gorbachev's new philosophy thus contributes towards building new bridges of understanding between the Soviet Union and the entire peace-loving humanity; between communists in the Soviet Union and democratic socialists and radical liberals in the rest of the world; between believers and non-believers within and outside the Soviet Union.

We in India discern a basic affinity between the fundamentals of Gorbachev's emerging world-view and the Gandhi-Nehru vision. We also identify in this affinity new possibilities of cooperation between India and the Soviet Union, both for pursuit of our enlightened national interests and for international objectives of a nuclear-free and peaceful world. We take special pride in the fact that Gandhi's principle of non-violence—which carries forward Buddha's teaching that real victory is one in which there is no victor and no vanquished—has been creatively absorbed by Gorbachev in his world-view. We also take special pride in the fact that Nehru's wise words that the goal of peace cannot be pursued by a warlike language reflecting the spirit of hatred and mental violence finds an echo in the Gorbachev approach to world problems. Like Nehru, Gorbachev affirms that the pursuit of peace requires a subtler mode of communication and a gentle language full of tolerance, understanding and compassion, and a willingness to understand each other's point of view. The cause of peace has to triumph by winning over the souls and minds of men and women.

No wonder that thoughtful and enlightened citizens all over the world welcome the Gorbachev proposals for a new dialogue. They contribute towards removing the vast distortions and deformations of socialism which were the products of Stalinist ideology and practice and which had created an almost unbridgable alienation of socialism from enlightened elements of human society both inside and outside the Soviet Union. Gorbachev is heading new creative forces and impulses of socialism which seek socialist renewal as a contribution to a new civilisation based on fresh affirmation of the humanist ideal.

9
Social Parasitism and Economic Development

In his essay on "Americanism and Fordism", Gramsci suggests that one of the important factors accounting for America's economic dynamism as contrasted with Europe was the absence of economically parasitic classes in the American society. Gramsci observed:

> Americanism, in its most developed form, requires a preliminary condition which has not attracted the attention of the American writers who have treated the problems arising from it, since in America it exists quite 'naturally'. This condition could be called 'a rational demographic composition' and consists in the fact that there do not exist numerous classes with no essential functions in the world of production, in other words, classes which are purely parasitic. European 'tradition', European 'civilisation', is, conversely, characterised precisely by the existence of such classes, created by the 'richness' and. complexity' of past history. This past history has left behind a heap of passive sedimentations produced by the phenomenon of saturation and fossilisation of civil-service personnel and intellectuals, of clergy and landowners, piratical commerce and the professional... army. (Antonio Gramsci, *Selections from the Prison Notebooks*, 1971, p. 281.)

This burden of parasitism as a brake on economic change and progress is far more significant in the case of ancient countries like India than it ever was in the case of European countries. *For India suffers from a double burden of a long history and a colonial past.* It has been aptly said by Gramsci again that the more historic a nation, the greater the burden that it carries of unproductive values and unproductive classes, of those who thrive, as it were, on "their ancestral patrimony" as "pensioners of economic history". India also carries the burden of a colonial past during which period parasitism struck deeper roots in the Indian social structure. And the deadweight of this legacy haunts us even now and thwarts the prospects of an economic renewal. And unrelenting fight against parasitism is possible only if the causal link between social parasitism and economic stalemate is clearly identified.

I

Economic development requires not only an attack on conspicuous consumption of upper classes but also a restriction of consumption appetites of all other classes. It requires as a first step, therefore, a sharp break from "social parasitism" without which neither the productive utilisation of existing economic surplus nor its enlargement can be effected. Social parasitism stands in the way of taking the next step of mobilising the productive classes for more work without their insisting on the immediate enjoyment of the fruits of this work.

Social parasitism can be defined as "a mode of existence based on extraction of wealth from producers without assisting them in any way to produce it."[1] The total divorce from economically productive activity constitutes, therefore, one essential aspect of parasitism. The most characteristic feature of a parasitic society, however, is that the parasitic classes enjoy a social and political supremacy over the productive classes; this results in denying the latter not only the resources for further development of productive activities but also the necessary psychological incentive for it. The parasitic orientation, far from confronting the disapproval of the total society, thrives at the cost of productive orientation. Parasitism, therefore, not only condemns productive activity to the status of drudgery, a routine, a misfortune; it also blocks innovation by channelising the flow of talent and energy towards parasitism rather than towards productive activity. The phenomenon of technical stagnation in parasitic societies is, therefore, not a chance occurrence but the logical results of social parasitism.[2] This assumes the form of a vicious circle insofar as parasitism keeps the flow of economic surplus to the productive sphere to the irreducible minimum, thus further restricting the scope for increase in production.

It is necessary to emphasise that this malady of parasitism may assume not only naked but also disguised forms. In fact, parasitism is more resistant to change in its disguised than in its naked form. The naked forms of parasitism are represented by the undisguised flow of the economic surplus into conspicuous consumption as in the case of the economically sterile landed aristocracy, the priestly castes and the feudalistic power elite. The subtle and disguised forms of parasitism are represented by those social classes which create the illusion of belonging to the economically and socially active categories of the population. In reality, however, they are neither making a direct nor an indirect contribution in a positive way to productive activity. One of the most harmful legacies of colonial rule is the continuing growth of these parasitic classes who appear in a non-parasitic garb.

II

An important characteristic of the underdeveloped and colonial countries like India is the over expansion of the "tertiary" sector. Thus the "sphere of circulation" grows in size without positively contributing to the "'sphere of production". This process results in the emergence of a significant social category represented by what may be called the "lumpen bourgeois."[3] To this class belong not only the moneylender, the trader in agricultural and non agricultural goods, the brokers and the intermediaries of various other kinds which thrive like mushrooms in a scarcity stricken economy. Explaining the genesis of this category, Baran aptly remarks:

> Where markets are as disorganised and isolated as they are in the underdeveloped countries, such (mercantile) profits are sought and

> found in an amazing variety of way. Real estate deals, exploitation of temporary and local short ages of various goods, speculation and arbitrage, brokerage fees for establishing contacts between buyers and sellers all yield sizable gains to the skilful operators in such transactions. The more or less chronic inflation in underdeveloped countries which gives rise to black-markets in foreign currencies, gold, and other valuables offers further opportunities for lucrative commerce, while the ever-present chance of procuring various concessions from government continually invites the resources, the energy and the ingenuity of well-connected and affluent men of affairs.[4]

This spectacular growth of a new type of parasitism creates an illusion of expanding economic activity without the reality of expanding economic productivity In fact, it constitutes a formidable barrier to genuine economic expansion in several ways. Insofar as it represents an intensified exploitation of the direct producers, it also represents a withdrawal of resources from the productive to the unproductive sphere. Insofar as the surpluses accruing from this source are ploughed back either in further expansion of the tertiary activities or in supporting a lavish style of living; it represents a significant drain on real capital accumulation and productive investment. But the most harmful effect of this new type of parasitism is that is brings discredit to the very idea of modern economic development. Economic expansion of this type does not permit the ideas of genuinely productive work and of the systemic acquisition of productive skills, values and the discipline of industrial life to strike roots and gain acceptance by the dynamic sections of society. The craze for "getting rich quick" through whatever means and methods stands in the way of the required re education of the society in the creative ways and norms of the industrial society. Baran has aptly observed that "the lumpen bourgeois' absorbing some of societies' most capable and dynamic individuals, at the same time wastes, corrupts, and destroys a vast quantity of what is perhaps one of the scarcest productive resources of all: creative human talent."[5]

If the "lumpen bourgeoisie" represents an actively Parasitic class, the "lumpen proletariat" is another category in underdeveloped countries which can be termed a passively parasitic class. It consists of those who are over-thrown from the traditional modes of production in agriculture and handicrafts but are left free floating without being absorbed into any modern mode of production or economic and social organisation. They represent not only a dependency dead weight on the economically active members of their families; they also constitute a fertile soil for retrograde ideologies (like communalism), a characteristic of socially and psychological uprooted groups. They provide the recruiting ground for hooligans, mastans and other types of functionaries of the underworld in big towns and cities.

And yet another form of massive but disguised parasitism exists in countries like India in the form of their proliferating bureaucracies and administrative establishments. The size of this establishment bears no relation either to the resource position of an underdeveloped country or to its basic needs and requirements. It is one of the colonial legacies continuing without any check on its indiscriminate expansion. In fact, as pointed out by Jawaharlal Nehru,[6] it has an expansionary momentum of its own even in the context of a slow moving society. This expansion is also fed by an out-of-date educational system which provides for unchecked expansion of higher education instead of providing for mass literacy, primary and secondary education with a strong production orientation. The very character of education with its elitist bias and divorce from production system has meagre relation to real needs and compulsions of a poor country. The system produces over whelming numbers of educated persons each year, most of whom neither seek nor achieve a genuinely productive career. These, however, constitute an important social stratum in coup gyres like India and a large section from it, if not the whole of it, can be characterised as the lumpen petty bourgeoisie. This class oscillates between total normlessness, on the one hand, and of misdirected energy and idealism, as in the case of Naxalites, on the other. Repository of vast, youthful vitality, this stratum lacks both the opportunities and the philosophical orientation to emerge as a creative force. As exemplified by Naxalism, it represents the unrealised promise of the new society as well as the severest indictment of the existing system.

Thus, whether, it is the "lumpen bourgeoisie", the "lumpen petty bourgeoisie" or the "lumpen proletariat "these three basic categories of an underdeveloped society exemplify the enormity of the problem posed by the parasitic way of life. They are products of a situation when the disintegration of the old society has occurred faster, much faster, than the creation of the new society. These transitional classes, however, pose the most serious cultural, social and political challenge for the leadership in countries like India. They create great difficulty in mobilising the society for productive pursuits. They also pose the most formidable problem in the sphere of maintaining as well as strengthening social discipline which is one of the indispensable requirements from modern economic development.

III

The understanding of social parasitism constitutes a challenging area for scientific enquiry, an area which has been totally neglected by social scientists. It is an area which calls for a multi disciplinary approach. The question most relevant for us here can be formulated as follows:

> Should social parasitism be treated fundamentally as an economic problem which is a product of economic backwardness and which can only disappear after economic development has been achieved?
>
> Or, should it be treated as a socio political or political economic problem, related not only to economic backwardness but also to the existence of a deformed "class society" and to the dominance of the parasitic over the producing classes?
>
> Or, should social parasitism be treated as a socio cultural or a social psychological problem .which may have originated in class society but which may continue to persist even after the abolition of the politico economic framework of a "class society"?

Let us first take up the economic interpretation of social parasitism. In an important speech to the members of the Indian Parliament in 1958, Gunnar Myrdal made a very perceptive formulation concerning, the economic basis of moral values.[7] He related the problem of social parasitism to the existence of cheap labour in Indian society. He argued that "not before labour has become an expensive commodity can we reach far with our social reforms".[8] He further observed that: "Respect in Indian society for manual labour will come when labour is not available in such almost scandalous surplus, when it is scarce and expensive. And when India will be far on the road to economic development".[9]

That there is some truth in Myrdal's argument is supported by the observed association between degree of labour scarcity and the intensity of social parasitism in different regions of India. It can be said that the greater the magnitude of cheap labour, the larger the scope for the practice of the most naked forms of social parasitism as in the eastern region of India. On the other hand, the sharper the trend towards labour scarcity, as in Punjab, the faster also is the decline at least of the most naked forms of social parasitism in that region. Myrdal's attempt to emphasise the dependence of moral and cultural phenomenon like social parasitism on an economic phenomenon like scarcity of labour is therefore not without some significance.[10]

In a perceptive essay, Andreski also propounds the thesis that "in a fairly complex society poverty fosters parasitism".[11]

What is the "social mechanism" through which poverty stimulates parasitism? In Andreski's view, the mechanism exemplifies "the principle of the least effort".[12] Men seek wealth both for the satisfaction of the basic needs and some also accumulate it in order to achieve more power and glory. If the easier road to accumulation of wealth lies through participation in productive activities, then men will choose this road and put their energies into such productive channels as offer the greatest economic rewards. Under conditions of poverty, however, men will be less inclined to put their energies into productive activities which are unrewarding; they will rather opt for parasitism and concentrate on forcibly appropriating from the producers of wealth as much of it as possible. In other words, "the energies which in an expanding economy will be applied to production, in a stagnant or contracting economy will be canalised into open or veiled predcation".[13]

Andreski's interpretation of social parasitism implies that the scope for social parasitism would be much greater in a stagnant and poverty stricken economy than in a dynamic and diversified economy. His analysis also implies that elimination of poverty may serve as a far more effective deterrent to social parasitism than any direct onslaught on this phenomenon.

No doubt the interpretations of both Myrdal and Andreski provide an insight into the economic roots of the phenomenon of social parasitism. But they do not distinguish sharply between the state of economic backwardness and the political economic framework of economic backwardness. And social parasitism even though not unrelated to the former is more immediately connected with the latter. Further, while the former can be tackled only on a long term basis, the latter can be drastically altered through social reform or revolution within a short period. Thus, even though it may not be possible to eradicate social parasitism as a phenomenon without eradicating poverty or economic backwardness, the scale of parasitism can be substantially reduced by altering the class structure and the balance of power as between the parasitic and the producing classes. Thus a backward society after a social revolution does not cease to be a poor society; but it does move towards being a predominantly non parasitic society.[14] That ideology, social consciousness and social organisation enable a society to shake off the deadweight of parasitism without yet being able to shake off the deadweight of poverty or economic backwardness is a phenomenon having profound significance for underdeveloped countries. This has the significance of a great social innovation for backward countries and this innovation has set in motion powerful cultural and political movements in these countries.[15]

It should be noted that Andreski's interpretation of parasitism is rooted in an evolutionary rather than revolutionary perspective. Instead of prescribing a direct attack on the economic and political dominance of parasitic classes, it relies more on inducing these classes towards a non parasitic orientation through manipulation of economic variables. For underdeveloped countries today, such an evolutionary course, however, is neither feasible from the political point of view nor even desirable from the point of view of rapid growth.

It should not be overlooked that there is a certain lag between the beginnings of economic growth, on the one hand, and the transition from parasitic to productive way of life, on the other. *For such a transition to be comprehensive, values have to be translated into norms, preferences into prescriptions, and principles of conduct into new social relationships.* This lag can be shortened or prolonged depending upon whether a country chooses a revolutionary or an evolutionary course.[16] Ire the latter case of slow adaptation of erstwhile parasitic classes of productive ways, there is not sharp break from parasitism. In fact, parasitism persists for a long time, slowing down the tempo of economic growth itself. The social history of many countries provides rich evidence not only of carry over parasitism even in the modern period, as in Germany, but even of retrogression into parasitism as in the case of Restoration post Meji Restoration Japan. On the other hand, in some other countries a drastic reform of the political economic structure created the prospect of a sharp break from parasitism and for affirming productive values. It also provided thereby more favourable conditions for the transition from a stagnant to a dynamic economy.

The underdeveloped countries today have no other option than to launch a direct attack on parasitism on the ideological and structural basis of its existence rather than wait for economic growth to ultimately take care of this problem. A sharp cultural confrontation between parasitic and productive values is as necessary for rapid economic transformation in these countries as a social and political confrontation between the parasitic and productive classes. It is important to note that ideological conflicts and power struggles in many under developed countries have not yet assumed the character of such a sharp confrontation between the producers and the parasites. It should also be emphasised that a conflict between exploiters and the exploited also becomes socially meaningful only when it evolves into sharp moral and cultural confrontation between parasitic and productive principles. Without this cultural motivation, any ideological conflict or power struggle ultimately degenerates into triviality and thus loses all significance as a creative force.[17] 'It can be said that the inadequate mobilisation for economic development in many Asian countries including India, is ultimately a product of an inadequate mobilisation against social parasitism at all levels by the leadership of these countries.

IV

It is important to note that in any country the index of a break from the mediaeval past is provided by the intensity of protest in that country against parasitism which constitutes the bedrock of mediaevalism in all societies. This protest is articulated first of all in the intellectual and cultural spheres. A vital feature of a genuine cultural renaissance, therefore, is the awakening of concern for the producing classes; this concern presupposes a moral revulsion against appropriating the fruits of labour without contributing to the labour process. A confrontation between parasitism and labour in this sense heralds the coming of the modern society.

In many underdeveloped countries, however, colonialism not only led to delayed industrialisation; it also led to the thwarting of a genuine cultural renaissance.[18] The middle class which was the product of colonial rule seldom emerged as a critic of social parasitism and as a crusader against it in many countries. Concern for the producing classes was, therefore, not central to the thought and practice of this middle class in countries like India. It should further be noted that in India, in spite of a plethora of radical ideologies, critique of parasitism and protest against its naked and disguised forms seldom formed the dividing line between the radicals and the conservatives. In fact, a clear cut ideology and programme of anti parasitism have seldom been the basis of a sharp ideological conflict or power struggle in the Indian national movement. *Seldom has the question of exploiters vs. exploited been also reformulated and enlarged into the question of parasitic vs. productive classes.* Even the critique of colonialism was seldom directed against the identification of colonialism with the parasitic classes of Indian society.

It may be recalled that Indian cultural renaissance in the pre Independence period occurred in the background of de-industrialisation rather than industrialisation. Further, quite often the leaders of this renaissance had themselves a parasitic background.[19] They came from classes alienated from the production process rather than from the producing classes, and they seldom made efforts to dissociate themselves from parasitism. Consequently, concern for the production principle and for the producing classes seldom crystallised in pre Independence India either into a cultural movement or a political mobilisation against parasitism.

It must be recognised, however, that Gandhi alone is exceptional figure in India's recent history, he stands out as the only crusader against parasitism and supporter of productive values.[20] Gandhi's concepts of "voluntary poverty", "non-possession" and "bread labour" represented in intellectual effort to provide a philosophical basis for non parasitism. By using these concepts as guiding principles of his daily life, he tried also to provide the model of a non parasitical life. In this way he made a valiant effort to pull out the Indian elite from its parasitical moorings. But non parasitism which was exemplified in Gandhi's personality did not survive beyond his lifetime; not a trace of it remained in the political sphere after Gandhi was removed from the Indian scene. The ingredients of Gandhi's thought and practice relating to non parasitism were over shadowed by its less basic ingredients. In fact, they perished without developing either into an effective philosophic critique of parasitism or into a powerful protest movement against it. It was but natural, therefore, that the end of colonial rule and the achievement of Independence did not coincide with a vigorous onslaught on parasitism and with the strong affirmation of productive values. If the colonial structure had buttressed more crude and naked forms of parasitism, independence vastly enlarged the scope for less naked but more stubborn and pernicious forms of parasitism.

This is not to deny that a certain degree of anti parasitism did gain strength in India following Gandhi's leadership of the national movement. This is also not to deny that a vague anti-parasitism did become a part of national consciousness; and in response to this consciousness, certain items of policy directed against the more naked forms of parasitism (for example, abolition of zamindari and jagirdari tenures) were incorporated in the national economic programme. As a result of these compulsions, the Indian ruling elite did undertake some measures in order to curb certain types of parasitism associated with colonial domination. It is also perhaps not an exaggeration to suggest that productive orientations and activities were provided a much more favourable framework during quarter of a century of freedom than during the entire period of colonial rule.

However, Independence did not mark a decisive break from the parasitic to productive orientations in all spheres of national life. It even enlarged the scope of parasitism as a result of a new factor, namely, the transfer of state power from foreign to native hands.

V

Independence opened up multiple possibilities of the use of State power it could be used for promoting either parasitic or productive activities. Thus state power could serve either as an instrument of what Andreski calls the "parasitic involution"21 of the economic system or it could serve as the propeller of the economy in a productive direction. By "parasitic involution of capitalism" Andreski refers to "the tendency to seek profits and to alter the conditions of the market by political means in the widest sense of that word".[22] In contrast, one can speak of a "productive" orientation where there is reliance for acquiring wealth on the economic mechanism of better utilisation of resources. One speaks of parasitic involution where economic mechanism is rejected in favour of other mechanisms like capturing influencial positions in politics, civil service, or army. The use of these position for acquiring wealth may be highly profitable but it is unproductive insofar as it is aimed at grabbing, a higher share of given wealth through open or disguised coercion rather than at increasing the wealth.

Parasitic involution, therefore, represents an enormous waste; and more serious is its role as a built in depressor of productive activities which are exposed to parasitic extortions. It ultimately condemns an economy to a low level of utilisation of economic resources.[23]

Even though independent India did not represent the classic case of parasitic involution of capitalism, parasitism has continued to be a chronic feature of Indian capitalism after Independence. Indeed a new feature was added to it, the parasitic involution of Indian socialism.

Studies on India's development after Independence have provided considerable evidence pertaining to "parasitic involution" of Indian capitalism. In fact, certain crucial features of India's economic situation after Independence assume meaning and significance if they are interpreted in terms of the concept of parasitism. That the transfer of State power to Indian hands has been instrumental in the drift of capitalism into parasitic channels can also be confirmed by recent studies of the Indian economy. This phenomenon is visible to the naked eye in the transformation of the dwarf size business houses at the time of

Independence into economic giants within a short period of two decades. It would be wrong, however, to regard this gigantic expansion of business houses as an indicator of the country's progress towards industrialisation. This expansion represents to a considerable extent the fruit of parasitic involution rather than that of productive orientation.

The diversion of public funds towards what Bettelheim calls "pseudo industrialisation",[24] rather than "true industrialisation" (that is, the expansion of industries producing luxury goods or consumer goods of secondary importance), the immobilisation of large proportion of the economic surplus into the spheres of commerce, moneylending and speculation offering high returns— these characteristics of the Indian business class fully exemplify its parasitic bias rather than its productive orientation. The frequent official investigations directed at individual members of the big business class, the official high level enquiries on the questions of corruption, of black money, or tax evasion and other malpractices in business spheres all these provide abundant proof of the massive use by big business of extra economic means for economic advancement.[25] They also testify to the fact that the big business in India has not evolved any conception of the ethics of business; it has not yet reached the stage of seeking profits within the constraints imposed by the good of the community as a whole.[26] It is yet far, very far, from evolving a business culture, and an appreciation of civic virtues. In other words, the big business is predominantly "parasitic" rather than "productive" in its basic motivations and commitments.

To make the picture complete, "the parasitic involution of capitalism" has to be seen in conjunction with "the parasitic involution" of Indian socialism. It should be noted that the political and bureaucratic elites, notwithstanding their commitments to a "socialistic pattern of society", have themselves been involved in parasitic extortion, though under the garb of pursuing socialist aims. This parasitism is also visible to the naked eye in the vast expansion of the state sector in the name of the socialist sector. The state sector is also a mixture of productive and non productive spheres, the non productive spheres often overshadowing the productive spheres. Even the productive spheres are run by a new technocratic and managerial elite which oscillates between productive work and parasitic extortion. The state sector has also been an instrument of parasitism insofar as it provides resources and support for expansion of those economic branches (like luxury goods sector),. which satisfy short term sectional interests rather than the overall long term needs of sustained economic growth. The political and bureaucratic elite has seldom used the instruments of power to curtail such forms of parasitism as the over expansion of the tertiary sector and the massive flow of resources into this sector. As Gadgil remarks, these decisions "relate more closely to profits of private groups than to national development policy".[27] It has, on the other hand, used state power to extract a high proportion of the national product for a small class at the top and allowed it to enjoy a level of living much higher than what is warranted by state of general poverty in the total society. (It is reported that if the total of housing investments during the first two Plans is taken to be about 11,000 millions rupees, eight or nine tenths of this sum—in all about 1.3 times the amount of industrial investments in the public sector during the Second Plan have been used for high class building construction.)[28]

It may not be an exaggeration to suggest that the top layers of the political, the bureaucratic and the business elites emerged as a powerful combination of vested interests dominating the state structure and using state power mainly for parasitic rather than productive aims. I*n this process the traditional distinction between the business elite, the political elite and the bureaucratic elite was very much obscured, if not obliterated.* The politicians and the bureaucrats assumed more and more the character of businessmen and the businessmen tended to encroach more and more into the spheres of politics and administration. We have earlier mentioned the absence of a business ethic or culture among the business elite. The above situation was also hostile to the development of an ethic or culture among the bureaucratic and political elites. The development of a social consciousness and a new culture are necessary concomitants as well as supports of a genuinely industrial society in its formative stages.

In this context Gunnar Myrdal has made an interesting contrast between Asian and European countries. He suggests "while it is, on the one hand, extremely difficult in South Asia to introduce profit motives and market behaviour into the sector of social life where they operate in the West that is, in the economic sphere it is, on the other hand, difficult to eliminate motivations of private gain from the sectors where they have been suppressed in the West the sphere of public responsibility".[29] A democratic structure, thus, presupposes a sharp differentiation of the business, the political and the bureaucratic elites; it also presupposes a high level of development of cultural values and norms characterising each type of elite. Underdeveloped countries like India, on the other hand, have been continuously subjected to internal and external pressures which tend to obscure the distinction between these elites; they also tend to retard the growth of ethical principles governing the conduct of each of these elite groups.

The phenomenon analysed above have sometimes been termed as "corruption," in both popular and scientific usage.

In our view the characterisation of this aspect of social reality as "corruption" does not bring out its significance as a major bottleneck in the economic transformation of countries like India. A different appraisal of "corruption" would be forthcoming if seen as a symptom of a much deeper malady, namely "parasitic involution" of both capitalism and socialism in India. Whatever be their ideological banner, in India the business groups wedded to capitalism and the political and bureaucratic elites wedded to socialism have all been guilty of following the easy road of amassing personal private wealth and fortune through political manipulation and extra economic devices; they have been less inclined to follow the hard road of acquiring more wealth through reorganisation of the production system and the enlargement of productive opportunities.

It is a paradox that a backward, poor and scarcity stricken society which can least afford the "parasitic involution", nevertheless offers the greatest scope for it both in the economic and the political spheres. It is not production for the masses here which offers the immediate scope for the highest profits; it is in the sphere of circulation that vast opportunities for immediate gain lie. The skills, inclination and traditions of the dominant economic groups which were divorced from production in the traditional economic order also strengthen the flow of entrepreneurial talent to this non productive sphere. *The lucrative heights of the economy are thus represented not always by the genuinely industrial but also by the non industrial spheres. Further, commanding heights of the economy do not lie entirely within the economy; they lie more and more within the political sphere.* The control of the instruments of state power thus becomes the most decisive factor for extending or. restricting the scope for economic gain. As the political sphere acquires a dominant-influence on economic life, *politics and administration themselves are converted into a vastly lucrative sphere.* Influential positions in the political and administrative spheres become an aid to parasitism into mutually reinforcing ways. Insofar as politics itself becomes "a strictly money making activity", it provides an unproductive channel for the dissipation of scarce human and financial capital. Thus, "capitalist groups spend large sums in politics.... Bribing officials, paying and arming supporters, buying votes, subsidising the press, bring reward in the shape of concessions, permits, appointments, contracts and the leniency of tax collectors."[30] The clandestine nature of such transactions does not permit a precise quantification of the vast sums involved in them, but that they represent a substantial drain of the investible surplus is without dispute.

This vulgar commercialisation of politics or the spurious politicisation of the economy does not always provide support to economic rationality; it supports the drift from rational considerations. It aids parasitism by setting in motion a process of diversion of scarce resources into non-productive or counter-production channels. The political and bureaucratic elites are enticed into formulating policies and taking decisions which encourage unproductive lines of economic activity; they play a major role in promoting expenditure of public funds for the satisfaction of sectional rather than social, short-term rather than long-term interests.

This relapse into parasitism on the part of the leading groups in society the political elite, the bureaucracy, the business class gradually sets the general trend for all sections of society. "Each one for himself and devil take the hindmost "this unbridled hedonism tends to become the guiding philosophy of a parasitism stricken society. The leading groups provide the model in this respect which other social groups specially the emerging groups tend to emulate. And the vast masses who fail to join this rat race and to benefit from it are driven into extremist and even subversive moods.[31] Parasitism of the elite thus causes a breakdown of the framework of social discipline.

Notes and References

1. Stanislav Andreski, *Elements of Comparative Sociology*, London, 1964, p. 227.
2. Ibid., Chapter 15.
3. Paul A. Baran, *Political Economy of Growth*, India, 1958, pp. 190-91.
4. Ibid., p. 190.
5. Ibid., p. 191.
6. See, "Administrative Jungle", *Jawaharlal Nehru's Speeches*, 1958, pp. 116-24.
7. Gunnar Myrdal, *Indian Economics Planning in its Broader Setting*, April 22, 1958.
8. Ibid., p. 16.
9. Ibid., p. 16.
10. It should be noted here that in his later writings Gunnar Myrdal has criticised the approach which considers social institutions, values and norms at superstructures dependent on an economic basis and which tackles the problem of changing the former not directly but indirectly by inducing changes in the latter. See, *Asian Drama*, Vol. III, p. 190.
11. Stanislav Andreski, op. cit., pp. 246-49.
12. Ibid., p. 248.
13. Ibid., p. 248.

14. In his *Letters from Russia*, Rabindranath Tagore shows a keen perception of the revolutionary transformation of the Russian social scene as a sequel to the disappearance of the leisured class. Russia after revolution, in his view, has not ceased to be poor but it has undoubtedly succeeded in imparting a new dignity to the poor. To quote: "It is because the distinction of wealth is non-existent here that the visage of wealth has changed; there is not the unseemliness of poverty, there is mere want."
15. It is important to note that both Gandhi and Mao Tse-tung made use of this discovery, the former though only partially and the latter with much greater thoroughness and consistency.
16. It is pertinent to recall here Marx's distinction between the two ways of transition from the feudal to the capitalist mode of production. The really revolutionary way is that "when the producer may become a merchant and a capitalist". The second way is that when "the merchant may take possession of production directly". Marx remarked that while the second way "serves historically as a mode of transition . . . nevertheless it cannot by itself do much for the overthrow of the old mode of production which it rather preserves and uses as its basis." (K. Marx, *Capital*, Vol. III, Foreign Languages Publishing House, Moscow, 1959). This second way is historically typified by countries like Germany, Japan and pre-Revolutionary Russia. The social and cultural concomitants of this type of development are summed up by Marx as follows: "Alongside of modern evils, a whole series of inherited evils oppress us, arising from the passive survival of antiquated modes of production with their inevitable train of social and political anachronisms. We suffer not only from the living but from the dead. (Karl Marx, *Capital*, Vol. I, Foreign Languages Publishing House, Moscow.)
17. This is the very essence of Gramsci's conception of "hegemony over the civil society". In his view, "the seizure of power by a new class is unlikely to succeed without a prior victory in the area of civil society; hence the struggle for hegemony, for cultural and moral predominance is the main task of Marxists in the advanced countries of the West". (Quoted in Commett, *Antonio Gramsci and Origins of Italian Communism*, Standford, p. 205). This task is perhaps more urgent in underdeveloped countries like India.
18. This point relating to the distorted character of Indian cultural re naissance and, in fact, to the perversion of Westernisation in India under colonialism has not been fully grasped by social scientists. It has been totally missed by V.S. Narvane (see Narvane's *Modern Indian Thought*, India, 1964).

It should be noted that D.P. Mukerjee comes closest to a realistic understanding of the weaknesses of Indian renaissance. But even he does not mention the lack of concern for producing classes or lack of awareness of the evil of parasitism as one of these weaknesses. (See, *Modern Indian Culture*, Bombay, 1942).

19. How far the revulsion against a parasitic way of life is expressed by Indian leaders in different phases of the national movement is an interesting point for investigation.
20. For some extracts from Gandhi's writings relating to non-parasitism, see, M.K. Gandhi, *Voluntary Poverty*, Navajivan Publishing House, Ahmedabad, 1961.
21. Stanislav Andreski, op. cit., pp. 250-57.
22. Op. cit., p. 250.
23. Op. cit., p. 251.
24. Charles Bettleheim, *Indian Independent*, Chapters IX and X.
25. See (i) *Santhanam Committee Report*, Government of India. (ii) *Report of the Commission of Enquiry* (Enquiry into the Administration of Dalmia-Jain Companies). (iii) Gunnar Myrdal, *Asian Drama*, Vol. I, Chapter 20, "Corruption and Its Causes", op. cit.
26. *The Monopolies Enquiry Commission Report*, Vol. I, draws attention to the fact that "big business has the power to corrupt and that the danger that power may be extensively used is not imaginary". It mentions "how some big businessmen do not hesitate to use their 'deep pocket' to try to corrupt public officials, in the attempts to continue and increase their industrial domain". They have not hesitated to use extra-economic devices to eliminate small competitors from the economic field. Further, big business is suspected even of "stretching its tentacles into the working of the very democratic machinery". (*Report of the Monopolies Enquiry Commission*, "Consequences of Concentration", Chapter VI).
27. See D.R. Gadgil, *Planning and Economic Policy in India*, India, 1961.
28. Charles Bettleheim, op. cit., p. 270.
29. Gunnar Myrdal, *Asian Drama*, Vol. II, p. 948.
30. Andreski, op. cit., p. 253.
31. For an insight into the factors underlying extremist and violent movements in the recent years, see, (i) Chand Joshi, "The Roots of Revolution", *The Hindustan Times, Sunday World*, November 7 and 14;1971; (ii) Chand Joshi, "Slums Boiling with Unrest," *The Hindustan Times*, September 15,1972; (iii) Jayaprakash Narain, *Face to Face*, Navachetan Prakashan, Varanasi, India, 1971.

10

Perspectives on Social Change: The Emergence of the Poor as a Class

> ...as long as they are at the beginning of the struggle, they see in poverty only poverty, without noticing its revolutionary and subversive aspect, which will overthrow the old society.
>
> The more a ruling class is able to assimilate the most prominent men of the dominated classes, the more stable and dangerous is its rule.
>
> —Karl Mark, *Capital*, Vol. III

The social situation in many Asian countries including India is marked by a great paradox. While the question of poverty has acquired political importance and legitimacy, the poor themselves are still far from becoming fully articulate and from emerging as a social force, i.e., as an agent of social change. There is still a vast hiatus between politicisation of the issue of poverty the politicisation of the poor. The issue of mass poverty is frequently used by one section of the ruling class for the indictment of the other sections without the poor themselves being mobilised to protest or revolt against their own deprivation.

I

What explains this lag between the vast mobilising potential of poverty and the lack of realisation of this potential for social and political change? What explains the emergence of the politics of poverty as an issue of power struggle within the ruling elite without the involvement of the poor themselves in the struggle against the forces perpetuating the socio economic basis of poverty? One must first seek the reasons for it in the contradictions of contemporary politics itself as reflected in the concern of the ruling elite for poverty but its distance from the poor. As a result, the issue of poverty is put into the centre of politics but the poor are not put at the centre of the political stage. Moreover, the spontaneous protests of the poor against their deprivation do not find adequate response from those who control the mass media (press, radio, TV, films etc.) or from those who dominate the political system (parliament, legislature, political parties, executive, judiciary and bureaucracy). Such a situation reminds one of the very perceptive observation made by Karl Marx in The Eighteenth Brumaire of Louis Bonaparte: "The bourgeoisie, to be sure, is bound to fear the stupidity of the masses as long as they remain conservative and the insight of the masses as soon as they become revolutionary" (Karl Marx, 1955).

Concern for poverty but distance from the poor is not only a marked characteristic of politics in countries like India. It is also a characteristic of journalism, literature and social science. Take journalism first which in the Western countries played a very important role in awakening social sensitiveness to the existence of the two nations, the rich and the poor, and which aroused social conscience in regard to the wide chasm between the two. The emergence of a social policy on poverty owes very much to the exposure of poverty by newspapers on a wide scale. In India itself in the pre-independence period newspapers played a very important role in bringing to limelight the conditions of the life of the poor. Journalism in post-independence India, however, has been characterised by preoccupation with life of elite and not the life of the masses. The free press has shown total insensitiveness to the life of the urban and the rural poor.

This is also true by and large of Indian literature. One may recall how in Western countries poverty and degradation of the working people in the early stages of industrialisation found its first poignant and indignant expression in the novels of Victor Hugo, Dickens, Zola and a host of other social novelists of the nineteenth century. But Indian literature has perhaps yet to throw up its Hugo, Dickens arid Zola voicing the suffering and degradation of the poor in India. It may be remembered that Munshi Prem Chand made an immortal contribution to Hindi literature by making the Indian peasant, oppressed by colonial and semi-feudal oppression, the central figure of his creative writing. There are, no doubt, a large number of novels by writers in all Indian languages depicting the social reality of rural India after the end of colonial rule. But post-independence Indian literature has yet to create a character comparable to Prem Chand's Hori!

If one considers the quality of Indian social science in terms of its sensitiveness to the existence of the poor, one finds social science much more deficient than literary writings. The performance of Indian social science is conspicuously dismal in sharp contrast to social science in the West in its formative period. It may be noted that in the West sociology had its origin in social surveys into the conditions of the poverty-stricken masses. Moreover, studies of the miserable conditions of the working people during the era of "primitive accumulation" served as a basis of the scientific as well as revolutionary writings of Karl Marx and F. Engels. Marx's *Capital* and Engle's *The Condition of the Working Class in England in 1844* drew upon the numerous surveys on the conditions of the poor to offer a comprehensive and trenchant indictment. of the social system responsible for accumulation of wealth at one pole and for immiserisation at another. Indian social science, however, has failed to mirror the life of the poor in India in any significant and meaningful way, even though naked poverty is fast emerging as the most conspicuous fact of Indian life as a sequel to the much faster dislocation of the old economic and social order than the creation of a new order.

Nothing in fact reveals so sharply the state of social science as the fact that *mass poverty provides the basis for many in the field of social science to get rich quick through poverty studies and poverty seminars financed by international and national agencies. Moreover, poverty experts travel round the world for seminars on poverty and unemployment without ever coming into direct contact with the poor.* Social science with a few exceptions thus provides a rich man's view of poverty and not the poor man's view. For the social scientist poverty is best understood when it is measured by "the poverty line", i.e., by impersonalised magnitudes of poverty. By these scientific devices and procedures refinement is achieved in measurements of poverty but insight is not provided into basic issues relating to the genesis of poverty or the relation of poverty to the social, economic and political system within which the poor are deprived. The very definition of poverty evades the basic issues of fundamental change in the system which generates and perpetuates poverty. Poverty is presented as if it is a marginal problem of an otherwise virile and vibrant system a problem which needs certain mechanisms and not a fundamental structural change.

Let alone the measurement-oriented and technocratic social scientist who writes about poverty but never comes into direct contact with the poor, even the fieldwork-oriented economists and social anthropologists have seldom made the poor the subject of their field investigations. Indian society has invested a vast amount of money, time and manpower in several dozen village studies by socialogists and social anthropologists. But the identity of the poor is lost, or the identification of the poor is completely obscured, by the failure of the social anthropologists to explore the fundamental division into haves and havenots and by their tendency to give exaggerated importance to the less fundamental forms of social stratification life caste which mystify this division between the haves and havenots. Social anthropologists have by and large ignored the role of caste as an ideological force obscuring the identity and crystallisation of the poor. The absence of any contribution by social anthropologists to poverty studies has not only impoverished social anthropology; the absence of a direct interaction with the people, which was central to the classical anthropological perspective, has also impoverished the very conception of anti poverty planning and mobilisation.

The gravest weakness of poverty studies and of antipoverty mobilisation is that they assign the crucial role in the crusade against poverty to the paternalism and the benevolence of the haves and their social and political representatives. But the poor are assigned no vital role in the fight against poverty. In other words, the greatest indictment of contemporary social thought and practice is that, to quote Karl Marx, "they see in poverty only poverty without noticing its revolutionary and subversive aspect, which will overthrow the old society"; they see in the poor only a helpless and pathetic human mass deserving pity and compassion of the ruling classes. Hence the endless discussions and deliberations of high-level experts and technocrats on schemes for the relief and uplift of the poor and on the best methods and means of implementing these schemes. What these sympathisers of the poor do not, however see, or do not wish to see, is the process of transformation of poor into the agents of social change. Social thought has still to put into forefront the question as to how from a position of being the victims of their fate the poor are converted into an active social force capable of overthrowing the old system which keeps them deprived. They emerge thereby as instruments of creating a new social system which would put an end to their alienation from the means of production and from the process of distribution of the fruits of production.

II

Past history of many countries shows that the transformation of the poor which from a passive human mass into a socially conscious, fighting class has been closely related to three important developments, viz., (i) the accentuation of "artificial poverty" in the midst of "natural poverty" as a sequel to the. growth of a market economy and capitalist economic order; (ii) the emergence of radical intellectuals as the creators and disseminators of a new outlook on poverty linking poverty with "exploitation" of direct producers by the masers of the means of production; and, (iii) the "emergence" of a critical consciousness among the poor as a sequel to the break from the fatalistic outlook and to a fundamental re evaluation of their position in society and their role in social change.

If one turns to past history one finds that the aggravation of "artificial" poverty was a necessary condition for the transformation of the poor into an agent of social change. "Artificial poverty" can be distinguished from "natural poverty" in two ways. Firstly, while the later is associated with a low level of development of productive forces, the former is the product of economic change and development itself. Secondly, under a regime of natural poverty, the conflict between the rich and the poor does not assume a naked form because of the mystification of this conflict by the institutions of caste, village community etc. With the emergence of "artificial poverty" the rich-poor conflict begins to assume a more naked form. Exploitation under "natural poverty" is less naked because the poor exist as petty property owners. Under "artificial poverty" it becomes naked as the poor who have been expropriated from material property ruthlessly and thoroughly are reborn as mere sellers of labour power. The emergence of "artificial poverty" is, therefore, the process of transformation of the petty property owners into a property-less mass. For a long time, however, the growth of propertylessness runs much ahead of the growth of wage labour, thus indicating pauperisation without proletarianisation. In other words, the genuine proletariat may be overshadowed for a long period by the lumpen proletariat and this fact may be responsible for blunting the revolutionary potential of poverty.

It should be noted that "natural poverty" denotes a state of economic scarcity associated with underdevelopment of the economy or the social productive forces. Such underdevelopment of productive forces favours the acceptance of poverty as a natural phenomenon (i.e., as god-given and unalterable) and to be shared by both the haves and havenots alike. Under such a regime of general economic scarcity the essence of exploitation in the relations between the haves and havenots tends to get obscured by the appearance of interdependence. The conflict of interest gets subordinated to the harmony of interest imposed by the common struggle against natural economic scarcity. Even when exploitation is perceived, it is ignored by the havenots as a price to be paid by them for the security provided to them by the haves.

A sharp discontinuity is introduced into this social situation with the emergence of a money and market economy and with the growth of a capitalist economy which is the most advanced form of a market economy. The capitalist economy, according to Marx, forced upon society the recognition of "the identity between national wealth and the poverty of the people" (Karl Marx, *Capital*, Vol. I, p. 725). Further, "for exploitation, veiled by religions and political illusions, (capitalism) has substituted naked, shameless, direct, brutal, exploitation" (Karl Marx, 1955, p. 36). This capitalistic social situation compelled a redefinition of poverty. In place of "physical or material deprivation" resulting from underdevelopment as in the past, one encounters mass poverty, which, paradoxically speaking, was the product of "development" itself. The very process of development which generated affluence for the few simultaneously generated poverty for the many (C.T. Kurien, 1978, pp. 8, 77). Marx pointedly mentions the emergence of a new category of the poor, the "free labouring poor", as "that artificial product of modern society" which was the product of dissolution of the old society. This was to be distinguished from "the naturally arising poor" which were the product of the old pre-capitalist society (*Capital*, Vol. I, p. 760). The revolutionary potentialities of poverty are closely related in the Marxian conception to the emergence of the "artificially impoverished" as a new category of the poor as distinguished from the old category of the "naturally arising poor". To quote Marx:

> For it is not the naturally arising poor but the artificially impoverished, not the human masses mechanically oppressed by the gravity of society but the masses resulting from the drastic

dissolution of society, mainly of the middle estate, that form the proletariat, although as is easily understood, the naturally arising poor and the Christian-Germanic serfs gradually join its ranks (Karl Marx, 1957, p. 57).

According to Marx, the sharp demarcation of the "artificially impoverished" provides to radical philosophy its material weapon while the "artificially impoverished" find in radical philosophy their spiritual weapon for social change (Karl Marx, 1957, p. 57). In other words, "natural poverty" provides the soil for conservative philosophy oriented to status quo while "artificial poverty" provides a favourable soil for radical philosophy oriented to structural change. The idea of structural change does not grow into a social force as long as there is no nakedly deprived class which can serve as a vehicle of this idea. In Marx's words: "It is not enough for thought to strive for realisation. Reality must itself strive towards thought" (Karl Marx, 1957, p. 52). But the deprived class also does not become an agent of structural change as long as it has not an access to radical ideas.

It must be pointed out that there is often a time lag between change in the objective basis and a transformation at the subjective level. This lag is reflected in the emergence of "artificial poverty" as a pervasive phenomenon without the emergence of the poor as a socially conscious force capable of identifying "the roots of their misery" (Karl Marx, 1961, p. 241).

It should be noted that in real life the phenomenon of natural poverty arising as a result of general economic backwardness is often mixed up with the phenomenon of artificial poverty arising as a result of the capitalistic development. This intertwining of two qualitatively different types of poverty acts as a mystifying force, keeping the poor in darkness about the social genesis of poverty and thus thwarting their emergence as a socially conscious force. The revolutionary potential of poverty may continue to be unexploited, or insufficiently exploited, for social change if "the artificially impoverished" are overshadowed by "the naturally poor". This potential may also remain unexploited if the "artificially impoverished" continue to interpret their poverty in terms of categories of understanding characteristic of the previous era (e.g., religion, caste, village community etc.) In emancipating the minds of millions of "the artificially impoverished" from the myths and illusions of the era of undifferentiated natural poverty and in ideologically remoulding their minds, the role of radical intellectuals is crucial. They act as the carriers of a new consciousness of the radical potential of poverty and accelerate the transformation of the poor from mere victims of class exploitation into "grave diggers" of the very system of class exploitation.

III

It is necessary to emphasise the crucial distinction, as suggested by Marx, between conservative. and a radical approach to the problem of poverty. The former considers poverty as the outcome of a defective pattern of distribution of means of consumption (i.e., income) and, therefore, lays the primary emphasis on restructuring the pattern of income distribution without reference to the pattern of distribution of means of production. The latter, on the other hand, starts from the premise that "any distribution whatever of the means of consumption is only a consequence of the distribution of the conditions of production themselves" (Karl Marx, 1954) and any scheme of redistributing the means of consumption independent of the mode of production is bound to prove futile. Only that section of the poor which experiences in every moment of its social existence an acute perception of their complete alienation from the means of production has, therefore, a revolutionary attitude towards poverty or the potential of attacking poverty at its roots. The remaining sections of the poor who are drawn into the system of ownership of the means of production in howsoever partial and inconsequential a manner are handicapped from perceiving the true caused of their poverty. In *The Eighteenth Brumaire of Louis Bonaparte*, Marx characterised the small holding peasants as conservative in the sense that remaining in "stupefied seclusion within the old order they want to see themselves and their small holding saved and favoured by the ghost of the empire." He also saw their radical potential insofar as impoverished by the domination of capital, small holding peasants were forced "to strike out beyond the condition of their social existence" and seek in the urban proletariat "their natural ally and leader" (Karl Marx, 1955, pp. 337–38).

While demarcating Marx's approach from other approaches it should also be pointed out that a Marxist approach to the problem of poverty is at once a structural and a developmental approach. The roots of poverty are identified by Marx in the sphere of the economic structure and not merely in the manner of functioning of this structure. Changing the structure rather than merely influencing the functioning of the structure appears as a crucial characteristic of the Marxist strategy for eradicating poverty. At the same time, Marx was not an economic romanticist who believed that a structural transformation was by itself sufficient to abolish poverty. Structural change only abolishes artificial poverty which is the product of the capitalist class system but not natural poverty which is rooted in the low level of development of productive forces. In one of his most perceptive statements Marx expressed his view that "justice can never rise superior to the economic conditions of the time" (Maurice Dobb, 1947, p. 148). Structural change is a Marxian conception, therefore, not a culmination of the struggle against poverty but only its beginning. It can become a crucial step in the struggle towards abolition of poverty only if it is an instrument of capital accumulation (i.e., of economic growth). Structural change becomes an engine of capital accumulation if it serves as means of eliminating the gap between actual economic surplus and potential economic surplus and thus the means of enlargement of the size of the economic surplus and the mode of its utilisation for productive purposes (Paul A. Baran, 1957, pp. 25–48).

The Marxian perspective on poverty views the struggle against poverty not as a single leap from poverty to plenty but as a protracted struggle against nature, i.e., against the low level of development of productive forces. The abolition of "artificial poverty" through structural change becomes the initiator of protracted struggle against "natural poverty", i.e., against the low level of development of productive forces which is the ultimate cause of material poverty. The emergence of the "artificially impoverished" as a separate category assumes historical significance insofar as it provides the social instrument of initiating the struggle against "natural" poverty. In struggling for their own abolition as a separate category in the short-run, the class of the "artificially impoverished" create the socio-economic and political preconditions for the abolition of "natural" poverty itself in the long-run.

In the contemporary social situation in India this Marxian perspective which links up the struggle against poverty with structural change, on the one hand, and with capital accumulation, on the other, has great historical relevance. This perspectives departs on the one hand, from those idealogue who seek to cope with poverty without altering the pattern of distribution of means of production which generates and perpetuates poverty. It departs, on the other hand, from those remanticists who make no distinction between "artificial poverty" and "natural poverty" and who, therefore, detach the struggle against poverty from the historically necessary task of capital accumulation. What is required in India is a new unity between radical theorists who uphold an integrated perspective on poverty and growth and the "artificially impoverished masses" who need this perspective in their struggle for a new life. A meaningful struggle against poverty must, therefore, begin with a struggle against the current poverty of philosophy which "sees in poverty only poverty without noticing its revolutionary and subversive aspect which will overthrow the old society"

IV

Several studies highlight how the growing crystallisation of the "artificially poor" as a class is fast emerging as qualitatively a new element of the Indian social situation. That this is a new element of the social situation in many Asian countries is confirmed by a number of recent works. Out of the numerous studies financed by international and national agencies which mystify the phenomenon of poverty there are some exceptions like the ILO studies published on Poverty and Landlessness in Asia (1977) which sharply indicate the emergence of a new type of poverty accompanying substantial economic growth in many Asian countries. These studies sum up the main features of this poverty as follows:

(i) 'The most outstanding facts to be noted are the worsening distribution of income and the declining real income of the rural poor at least in a number of cases. Those studies which contain the relevant data show that the shares of the lower decile groups in aggregate income and consumption have been declining even during periods of rapid agricultural growth. These are significant differences from country to country as regards the proportion of population that has been adversely affected, but in each country for which data exist a substantial proportion of the lowest income groups appear to have experienced a decline in their share of real income over time. Indeed, the evidence from the case studies points to an even stronger conclusion.

In each case a significant proportion of low income households experienced an absolute decline in real income" (p. 9).

(ii) "The countries studied are all characterised by a highly unequal distribution of land ownership... . The continuation of highly unequal ownership of land during a period of rapid demographic growth has resulted in increased landlessness and near landlessness" (p. 11).

(iii) "The answer to the question why the poverty of the poorest groups of the rural population has increased has more to do with the structure of the economy than its rate of growth... . The initially high degree of inequality of income and wealth, the concentration of the economic surplus in few hands, and the fragmented allocative mechanisms constitute a socio economic context in which powerful dynamic forces tend to perpetuate and even accentuate low standards of living of a significant proportion of the rural population" (p. 22).

(iv) "Most of the poor are not unemployed and many of the unemployed are not poor... The movement of labour represents little more than a shuffling around of poverty. As long as the economic structure remains as has been described, with its income distribution and resource allocation mechanism intact, the major function of rural to urban migration is to spread the growing poverty of the countryside to the towns" (p. 25).

It is clear that the social situation in many countries of Asia has been undergoing a qualitative transformation with the emergence of a new type of poverty. This poverty is not "due to general stagnation of the economy" but due to an economic system in which vast masses are alienated from the property structure and the mode of production, and consequently from the mode of distribution of the fruits of production. The key to this poverty in spite of economic growth lies in the very nature of the economic system. In this new social situation an objective basis is emerging now for the comparatively sharper crystallisation of the poor as a nakedly deprived class than in the past. An objective basis is also emerging for greater unity of the rural and urban poor since the urban poor are in most areas rural poor pushed out into urban areas. The recent resurgence of Ruralism dramatising the rural-urban cleavage or of Casteism dramatising the caste disparities rather than the rich-poor cleavage is meant to a large extent to mystify and obscure the fast-growing class differentiation in the rural and in the caste communities.

In recent years numerous studies have drawn attention to the growing class differentiation within the peasantry and within castes without, however, assessing its significance for social and political movements. We refer to the findings of a few of these studies as illustrations of the tendencies of downward mobility within the upper castes and of upward mobility of social strata within the middle and the lower castes.

In a study on "Regional and Caste Factors in India's Development" K.N. Raj tried to analyse the data on caste and occupation as provided by the National Sample Survey. The results of which are very illuminating. While taking note of the imperfection of the data on caste and class, Raj offers the following findings from the available data:

> That there is a correspondence between 'caste" and 'class' at the two extremes appears to be thus borne out by the figures. But it is also clear particularly in the intermediate categories that class cuts across caste divisions. Thus nearly, 7 per cent lower caste households in the rural areas are 'farmer' households, and the number of lower caste households among the total number of 'farmer' households works out to well over 40 per cent... .
>
> Similarly, more than 18 per cent of the middle caste households, it would appear, were `agricultural labourers' and 'share croppers'. The number of rural Hindu households belonging to these two categories was 13.3 million of which the middle caste accounted for 2.2 million. Approximately one out of every six households occupied as agricultural labourers and share croppers in the rural areas belong to the middle caste group. (K.N. Raj, 1961, p. 111).

Unfortunately, no comparable data are available for the latter period to provide insights into changing class diffrentiation within caste over time. But on the basis of information available at. the micro level it is possible to suggest that the internal class differentiation within the upper, the middle and the lower caste has been intensified in recent years.

Srinivas's recent village study, The Remembered Village, takes note of the divergence of class from caste in the following words:

> There was a certain amount of overlap between the twin hierarchies of caste and land. The richer landlowners generally came from

such high castes as Brahmin, Peasant and Lingayat while the Harijans contributed a substantial number of landless labourers. But a few members of the low castes such as the Smith, Oilman and Toddyman owned reasonable amounts of land while several Peasants and Shepherds were without land. Such lack of overlap between the two hierarchies produced interesting consequences" (M.N. Srinivas, 1976, p. 169).

One finds Srinivas speaking of "conflicts between the rich and the poor" and "more effective exploitation of the poor" by the wealthy and the powerful of the village (p. 255) in the present work, while in his earlier village study he spoke mostly of high and low castes.

A sharper focus on the increasing divergence of class from caste is evident from Beteille's study of a Tanjore village. Beteille observes:

> In traditional society, and even fifty years ago, there was much greater consistency between the class system and the caste structure. One can even say, with some risk of oversimplification, 'that the class system was largely subsumed under the caste structure'.
>
> Over a large area of the agrarian economy, the traditional arrangement seems to have been thus: the Brahmin Mirasdars owned land which they leased to non-Brahmin tenants who had it cultivated by engaging Adi-Dravida labourers. This, of course, is a highly simplified picture, and even in the traditional economy there were exceptions to the simple correspondence between Brahmin and landowner, non-Brahmin and tenant, and Adi-Dravida and agricultural labourer. These exceptions have increased considerably over the last fifty years. This class system can no longer be seen simply as an aspect of the caste structure (Andre Beteille, 1966, pp. 191, 195).

Beteille has drawn attention to downward mobility among the Mirasdars and the upward mobility among the non-Brahmin peasants and Adi-Dravida labourers. He pointedly mentions those "upward-moving non-Brahmin peasants" who have acquired the status of landowners and Adi-Dravida and labourers who have become tenants or acquired ownership of small parcels of land (pp. 194–98). Noting the differentiation in tenancy, he draws attention to "tenants with big leases who may identify themselves more closely with landowners than with small peasants" (p. 207).

Analysing the changes in the role of caste in the village economy Kathleen Gough's Caste in a Tanjore Village notes how "the caste community is no longer homogeneous in occupation and wealth" and how "caste is today a limiting rather than a determining factor in the choice of occupation" (K. Gough, 1971, p. 32). She also draws attention to economic polarisation among Brahmins as indicated by "some owning up to 30 acres of land and others as little as 3 acres". Moreover, she also takes note of the economic heterogeneity among non-Brahmins: "among 43 non-Brahmins who remain in agriculture or horticulture three are small minor cultivators, nine are Pannaiyals contracted by the year, ten are daily coolies, and twenty-one lease land on Kuthakai tenure" (p. 32). Similarly, those low castes who have remained in agricultural labour are highly stratified. Only 22 per cent are now Pannaiyals. Thirty-eight per cent have in the past become kuthakai tenants on the same terms as non-Brahmins while thirty-nine per cent have become daily coolies and one man has risen to the status of a small owner cultivalor. (p. 32).

Gough offers the following assessment of the evolving social situation:

> In Tanjore villages in 1952, indeed, one major conflict over rode all others: that between the landed and the landless. It results from acute agricultural over population, the concentration of land ownership within a small fraction of the population, and the failure to develop industrial employment for surplus villages. It seems logical to conclude that such economic and class conflicts, whatever their outcome, will in the future weaken the identities of caste (cough, 1971, p. 59).

Another village study of Thaiyur Panchayat (Tamilnadu) sums up the caste-class nexus in the following words:

> There is a strong but far from perfect correlation between caste and class: 18 per cent of the non-Harijan households belong

> to the upper class of big farmers, while only 3 per cent of the Harijan households do. This implies that the traditional relations of production which always involved members of different castes in antagonistic positions still largely persist.... But in terms of absolute numbers, class of big farmers consists of more Harijan households than non-Harijan ones. This implies that members of the same caste meet in relations of exploitation, and since this is at variance with the caste ideology, we can also expect changes in the ideological universe. The Harijan predominance in the class of middle farmers is likely to work in the same direction. There is a sizable group of Harijans who no longer are poor and exploited, and whose economic position contradicts their impurity. The economic position of the Harijans is no longer homogeneous, but since the heterogeneity must be accounted for we expect to find a new ideology which encompasses all aspects of Harijan experience (G. Djurfeldt and S. Lindberg, 1976, pp. 216–17).

We have deliberately drawn upon village studies mostly from South India because the overlap between caste and class was reported to be the closest in this part of the country. The divergence of class from caste, therefore, emerges very sharply from studies of the changing villages relating to this part. One can, however, refer to caste studies relating to other parts which reveal the same tendencies.

Anand Chakravarty's study of a Rajasthan village reveals that the new landowning class is no more identical with the Rajput caste. Thus, as a consequence of downward mobility among the Rajputs and upward mobility among non-Rajput castes, the landowning class is now multi-caste in composition. The broadening of the landowning class has been associated with class differentiation within the upper, middle and the lower castes (Anand Chakravarty, 1975, pp. 96–98).

Another outstanding work which throws light on the transition from caste to class is Jan Breman's study of South Gujarat villages called *Patronage and Exploitation* (1974). Breman characterises this process as "depatronisation" of relationships between the dominant landowning castes, on the one hand

and the labouring castes, on the other. He shows the close link between "depatronisation" or the transition from "patronage" to exploitation "as a changeover to a capitalist mode of production" (Breman, 1974, p. 253). He notes that "the contrasts in the rural regions between the weakest and the strongest party have sharpened" as indicated by open forms of "large scale rural pauperisation" (p. 255). He considers this as a qualitatively different situation: "To the conclusion that exploitation was inherent in the hall system, and that patronage may occur in a situation of exploitation should be added the comment that the difference between past and present is more than one of degree" (Breman,1974, p. 225).

Another significant aspect of Breman's study is that it also shows the transformation of the rural poor into the urban poor. The rural poor contribute to the "emergence of the informal sector" in the urban economy.

Breman observes:

> And yet the attempt of the village population to break out of the rural system into non-agrarian fields cannot be explained by the magnetic effect of the district town and other employment centres: its main cause is expulsion from the agricultural economy. It is not merely the result of population growth in which an increasing supply of labour eventually becomes a surplus. There have also been changes in the mode of production in agriculture which have led to a redefinition of labour utility... .
>
> The fact that it is impossible to accommodate the available labour force within this sector has led to a situation in which a steadily increasing proportion of the rural population is compelled to seek a living outside agriculture or at least to find a complementary income (Jan Breman, 1977, p. 173).

Breman's study yields insights into the objective basis as well as the subjective perception of poverty. One finds that "depatronisation" and impersonalisation of economic relationships is leading the rural poor increasingly to "a collective awarencess of their condition of subjection, a feeling of being wronged and the beginning of an attempt at collective opposition against their exploiters" (p. 230). Breman adds at once that "the conditions that are a pre requisite to implementing their protest organisationally in an effective way are lacking" (p. 230). In other words, the potential strength of the poor is enormous but their actual bargaining or striking power is extremely limited. Breman's analysis of why the revolutionary potential of poverty does not get realised is very illuminating. To quote:

> From various parts of India there have recently been reports of agricultural labourers who are beginning to offer resistance against the exploitation to which they are exposed.
>
> The horizontal ties among the Dublas (the labouring groups) have remained weak. Some are more oppressed than others. As share croppers, servants, casual labourers, and gang labourers they have no parallel interests. The limited favours that can be obtained in a situation of extreme and continuing scarcity situation lead (again) to patronagelike relationships. An attitude of protest, for instance, is incompatible with the need of showing oneself worthy of consideration by behaving "well". Intra-class antagonism manifests itself in dissension and mutual watchfulness. If someone refuses to work for one rupee, another is always prepared to take his place.... In the situation of poverty there are undoubtedly elements that constitute obstacles to mutual solidarity (p. 257).

While taking note of this inhibitive aspect of poverty in the short-run, Breman highlights the social dynamics of poverty under capitalism which in the long run unifies and activises the poor. To quote:

> It is the aggregate of inequality economic and political–along with social polarisation that forms the basis for a growing collective perception of injustice, even if fear of sanctions usually limits any expression of it to verbal avowals during encounters in their own hamlets. Indeed their awareness of hamlets is further stimulated from outside because Anavils (the landowning class) regard all the Dublas being cut from the same cloth. The landlords are strikingly uninformed about anything concerning their labourers, including

> the contrasts among them, and what is more, they are totally indifferent to them (p. 257).

Sociologists have drawn attention not only to the trend of class differentiation in villages and in castes but also to the transformation of castes into political factions. Leach has argued that such political role of caste is "a defiance of caste tradition" which may "not be clear either to the actors or to the anthropological observer" (Leach, 1971, p. 6). He has, however, not clarified whether the emergence of caste lobbies helps the rich or the poor of the caste groups. Andre Beteille has. provided an insight into the exploitation of caste loyalties as an instrumentality for furtherance of their class interests by the top groups of the emerging agrarian hierarchy. To quote:

> Thus, the top of the emerging agrarian hierarchy consists of a set of individuals having certain common social and economic properties, linked together in loose-knit networks and becoming increasingly aware of their common economic and political interests. Those at the top have advantages of both resources and skills. Sociologically the most distinctive feature of the progressive farmers is that they combine ownership of land and capital with skills in manipulating both 'traditional' and 'modern' institutions" (A. Beteille, 1974, p. 112). He thus calls this new class 'ambidextrous' and notes "the decline of the community" as consequence of the consolidation of this new class (p. 105).

V

It can be seen from above that the revolutionary potential of poverty would be obscured if the question of rich vs. poor is misrepresented as a question of town vs. the village or of caste vs. caste. It is idle to think that poverty in the rural areas can be fought without the support of the urban poor and that rural development can be achieved without the support of urban industrial development. It is also idle to think that the poor of one caste can secure an enduring advance in their material condition without unity with the poor of the most oppressed caste who stand opposed to exploiting the idea of caste for dividing poor and thus thwarting the process of their transformation into an agent of social change. Town vs. village and caste vs. caste, therefore, ultimately helps in perpetuating system-generated poverty.

Ruralism and Casteism in the above background perform the ideological function of mystifying the real process. They provide to the new rural elite the banner for agitation with a view to extraction of more resources in the name of the rural community and of backward castes. The enhanced resources are, however, used not for mass-oriented development but for strengthening the interests of dominant groups in the village and of dominant sections in the "backward castes". They provide the ideological cover under which the emerging power-elite in the village resorts to intensified and ruthless exploitation of the rural masses in new ways. In short, in presentday India Ruralism and Casteism are the most formidable obstacles in transforming poverty into an agent of social change.

Notes and References

1. Karl Marx, *Capital*, Vol. I, Moscow, 1955.
2. Karl Marx and F. Engels, *On Religion*, Moscow, 1957.
3. Karl Marx, *Selected Writings in Sociology and Social Philosophy*, Edited by T.B. Bottomore and M. Rubel, 1961.
4. Karl Marx and F. Engels, *Selected Works*, Vol. I, Moscow, 1955.
5. Karl Marx, *Critique of the Gotha Programme*, Moscow, 1954, p. 57.
6. F. Engels, *The Condition of the Working Class in England in 1844*, London, 1950.
7. Pawl A. Baran, *The Political Economy of Growth*, New Delhi, 1953.
8. C.T. Kurien, *Poverty, Planning and Social Transformation*, New Delhi, 1978.
9. Gunnar Myrdal, *The Challenge of World Poverty*, 1970.
10. International Labour Office, *Poverty and Landlessness in Rural Asia*, Geneva, 1977.
11. Ajit Roy, *The Economics and Politics of Garibi Hatao*, Calcutta, 1973.
12. V.M. Dandekar and N. Rath, *Poverty in India*, Indian School of Political Economy, Bombay, 1971.
13. B.S. Minhas, *Planning and the Poor*, New Delhi, 1976.

14. V.I. Lenin, 'To the Rural Poor', *Collected Works*, Vol. 6, Moscow, 1961.
15. K.S. Shelvankar, *The Problem of India*, 1940.
16. W.F. Wertheim, *Evolution and Revolution*, 1974.
17. E.M.S. Namboodiripad, *The Economics and Politics of the Socialist Pattern*, New Delhi, 1966.
18. M.K. Gandhi, *Selections from Gandhi*, Edited by N.K. Bose, Ahmedabad, 1957.
19. R.H. Tawney, *The Radical Tradition*, 1964.
20. R.H. Tawney, *The Acquisitive Society*, 1966.
21. Jawaharlal Nehru, *On Socialism*, New Delhi, 1964.
22. Frantz Fanon, *The Wretched of the Earth*, 1963.
23. Maurice Dobb, *Soviet Economic Development Since 1917*, Cambridge, 1947.
24. Andre Beteille, *Studies in Agrarian Social Structure*, Delhi, 1974.
25. P.C. Joshi, "The Remembered Village, Bridge between Old and New Social Antrhopology", *Contributions to Indian Sociology*, 1977.
26. M.N. Srinivas, "The Social System of a Mysore Village", in McKim Marriot (ed.), *Village Indian Studies in Little Community*, 1961.
27. M.N. Srinivas, *The Remembered Village*, Delhi, 1976.
28. E.R. Leach (ed.), *Aspects of Caste in South India, Ceylon and North-West Pakistan*, 1971.
29. K. Gough, "Caste in a Tanjore Village", E.R. Leach (ed.), *Aspects of Caste in South India, Ceylone and North-West Pakistan*, 1971.
30. K.N. Raj, "Caste and Regional Factors in Economic Development" in J.C. Daruvala, *Tensions in Economic Development in South East Asia*, 1961.
31. G. Djurfeldt and S. Lindberg, *Behind Poverty: The Social Formation of a Tamil Village*, Student, 1975.
32. Andre Beteille, *Caste, Class and Power*, Bombay, 1966.
33. Anand Chakravarty, *Contradiction and Change*, Delhi, 1975.
34. J. Breman, *Patronage and Exploitation*, 1974.
35. J. Breman, "Labour Relations in the Formal and Informal Sectors: Report of a Case Study in South Gujarat, Part I", *The Journal of Peasant Studies*, Vol. 4, No. 3, April 1977.

Index